Toward a Kinder, More Compassionate Society:
Working Together Toward Change

From the 2022 WECAN
Early Childhood Educators Conference

Contributions by
Meggan Gill, Keelah Helwig, Joaquin Muñoz, and Others
Edited by Susan Howard

Waldorf Early Childhood Association of North America
Spring Valley, New York

Toward a Kinder, More Compassionate Society:
Working Together Toward Change

ISBN 978-1-936849-58-1

Cover image: Courtesy Silvia Jensen
Published in the United States by
The Waldorf Early Childhood Association of North America
285 Hungry Hollow Rd.
Spring Valley, NY 10977
+1 845-352-1690
info@waldorfearlychildhood.org
www.waldorfearlychildhood.org

For a complete book catalog, contact WECAN or visit our online store at
store.waldorfearlychildhood.org

This publication is made possible by a grant
from the Waldorf Curriculum Fund.

Contents

Introduction

Susan Howard

Over the course of three years, the Waldorf Early Childhood Association of North America (WECAN) has focused its annual conference activity on the theme "Toward a Kinder, More Compassionate Society." In 2021, nearly nine hundred Waldorf early childhood educators from North America and around the world participated in our first online conference. This event was a historic moment in our collaborative work toward greater diversity, inclusion, equity, and access in our movement. We centered our colleagues who are Black, Indigenous, and people of color, and for the first time, we invited a keynote speaker from outside the Waldorf movement, Laleña Garcia, who launched us into a whole new exploration of our work with ourselves and with our children.

In 2022, our work on the conference theme continued. Stimulated by Laleña's lively and inspiring presentation on working with Black Lives Matter principles in a non-Waldorf setting, we explored how to translate this into our work as Waldorf early childhood educators. Keynote speakers Meggan Gill, Keelah Helwig, and Joaquin Muñoz engaged in conversations encompassing the essence of our work and deepening our understanding of place-based education and the trappings of cultural appropriation. Nearly eight hundred Waldorf early childhood educators participated in the conference, which was a significant step in our working together toward change and toward the kinder, more compassionate society we all know is possible.

In this volume, we have collected notes from the keynote presentations and workshops from the 2022 conference as resources to extend and share the learning that took place.

A wholehearted thank you to everyone who contributed to the inspiring 2022 conference, and especially to the following:

- Otsistohkwi:yo for sharing the Haudenosaunee thanksgiving address
- Meggan Gill, Keelah Helwig, and Joaquin Muñoz, for their stimulating, eloquent collaborative keynote sessions
- Silk and String Puppeteers from Toronto and members of the Everlasting Tree Community for their puppetry performance of the legend of the Dancing Stars
- Lynn Turner and Leslie Wetzonis-Woolverton for facilitating the Q&A and the closing session and post-conference Listening Space
- Anjum Mir, Laura Mason, and Magdalena Toran for joining Lynn and Leslie to sound the notes from the conference and look toward our future work together
- Members of the Ak Lu'um Community School for the singing and marionette performance of "The Blue Deer," a Huichol legend
- All the workshop presenters who shared their gifts and ongoing research and practice with conference participants
- The incredible WECAN conference team, whose work behind the scenes made it possible for us all to come together in this unique way.

With gratitude,

Susan Howard
WECAN Coordinator
September 2022

Accountability Statement

The 2021 WECAN Board

We formed as an association of colleagues in 1984. Since that time, to the great detriment of all, children, families, and colleagues throughout our movement who are Black, Indigenous, people of color, and members of the LGBTQ+ community have not been fully seen, respected, welcomed, and affirmed in our classrooms and communities.

The WECAN board acknowledges this harm, the loss it has caused, and the opportunity we are now afforded to honestly examine and renew the work of our organization. This will include examining our practices and biases, listening, inquiring, and growing into a fuller understanding of race, class, and gender in North America in the twenty-first century.

Knowing better does not change what has occurred, but in awakening there is the possibility to participate in the more beautiful world we know is possible.

As the leadership of WECAN, we as board members take accountability for the pain that has been caused throughout our North American Waldorf early childhood community. We recognize that in order to fulfill the mission of Waldorf education in the next century, we must transform our practices out of an expanded awareness of bias in race, class, and gender and the particularities of each child's and family's uniqueness.

To educate our children in and toward freedom we must understand not only the developmental needs of children but also the context of the society and structures that influence them and us.

Our acknowledgement of accountability is not out of guilt, but out of our deep, ongoing commitment to children, families, and colleagues, and to the evolution of Waldorf education as a force for social change. We take this step of accountability as a loving act toward self and community that allows for new courage and wisdom and honors our responsibility for one another.

To this end the WECAN board has committed to:

- Ongoing personal and collaborative commitment to unmask and transform systemic racism and cultural, gender, and class biases that impede our work
- Diversifying the WECAN board and examining our board practices through the lens of white dominant culture
- Expanding and activating our WECAN Inclusion, Diversity, Equity and Access (IDEA) Committee, populated by Black, Indigenous, people of color, and white colleagues
- Creating and implementing our WECAN Diversity Statement
- Collaborating with other anthroposophical organizations on inclusion, diversity, equity, and accessibility within the movement
- Reviewing and renewing our teacher training practices in the light of IDEA
- Hosting and promoting professional development opportunities such as the 2022 conference and the activities that will take place afterwards to extend the learning that we are all engaged in.

As a board we see this as a living process, and we welcome your insights and reflections now and into the future.

As Waldorf early childhood practitioners, we are invited to develop the spiritual attributes of greatheartedness, humility, curiosity, interest, wonder, and integrity. In these unique and challenging times, we are being asked to see clearly, without any veil of illusion, what influences us. We are being asked to be willing to change, to respond, and to transform.

This is potent, painful, powerful, essential work. With collaborative, sensitive, and honest activity, we can go forward together.

Adrienne Doucette, Anjum Mir, Gabriela Nuñez-Plata, Heather Church, Holly Koteen-Soulé, Keelah Helwig, Louise deForest, Magdalena Toran, Nancy Blanning, Ruth Ker, Sarah Arnold, and Susan Howard

On Sensing Each Other, Ourselves, and the World:

Excerpts from the WECAN 2022 Keynote Address

Meggan Gill, Keelah Helwig, and Joaquin Muñoz

In February 2022 WECAN convened its annual conference with the theme "Toward A Kinder More Compassionate Society: Working Together Toward Change." The keynote address was a collaborative and relational effort by Meggan Gill, Keelah Helwig, and Joaquin Muñoz. The excerpts below offer an overview of the keynote addresses themselves, organized by day and by theme. Part one is "Sensing Each One," part two is "Sensing Ourselves," and part three is "Sensing the Future."

Sensing Each One:
Attuning to the Needs of the Moment

Keelah

We love being wrapped in the sweet embrace of story. It is a place where Waldorf education weaves perfectly into our various cultures. We are story people, and it is out of that rich tradition that we invite you to receive our stories. We share our biographies in an effort to model vulnerability, to bend this screen, to lean in and create connections. We offer them as entry points into the conversations that will unfold during the course of this weekend. We invite you all to listen deeply with your whole heart. Our stories are beautiful, hard, tender, infuriating, illuminating, and truer than true. They can be hard to hear. They are hard to tell. They are offered as gifts, with a hope that they are received in the manner we intend.

Meggan

I'd like to begin by sharing something that arises out of my exploration of what it could mean to "decolonize" myself. I like the language that some people are using: "undoing settler-colonial culture." I recognize that I was raised in the settler-colony of British Columbia, Canada and that within my DNA lies six generations of information regarding my survival. I am particularly focused on how this affects my self-expression in the world of language, speech, and writing. I have other forms of self-expression, more liberating for my experiences of being Black and queer, that find their place on the dance floor or in the karaoke room. Self-censoring or filtering our words and expressions in our modern-day world is indeed necessary if we want to move through the world being both respectful and respected. However, as I consider my family biography, my place on the social wheel of power and privilege, and the generationally, genetically inherited forms of internalized oppression, I must also question my information about how these measures of respect are affecting me.

Black Americans have no choice but to continually imagine a better world for our children. It has, in fact, become an inherent understanding in how we raise our children, shape their developing identities, and share family biographies, knowing that whatever comforts or freedoms we may or may not be experiencing now have been acquired through hard work, sacrifice, faith, and diligence. We want to equip our children with the strength to endure the truth, the confidence to overcome adversity, the spirit to protect them from the pain. Basic rights to safety, security, acceptance, and to life itself are still, today, not a given that many Black parents can afford for their children. The obvious statement *Black Lives Matter* still needs to be heard over and over, because it is still not a reality. *#sayhisname*

When we talk about our Indigenous peoples, we need to acknowledge that the genocide has never ceased. For many, the evidence of this is literally being unearthed from the institutions that stole and kept children, "schooling them" to become more like European settlers, erasing languages, names, customs, and identities. I have experienced a form of this in my own family biography—so much so that my son and his cousins have little to no access to our Indigenous family's place of origin, culture, or history, even though I am not speaking of a far off, distant relative; I am speaking of my great-grandmother. Acknowledging this is sad, but also liberating because it's the truth. Otherwise, the dominant culture will persist and where there should be a thread or story or a root, there would be nothing. We need to give back what we have taken. *#landback*

When I think of the progress that has occurred during my lifetime for the queer community, I am pleased to say that I, as a queer lesbian in an interracial marriage, have the right to marry, receive my spouse's benefits, and am protected, in theory, from legal discrimination. However, I am acutely aware of the high rate of violence and death that continues to affect trans and gender expansive communities, and furthermore, that lawmakers are persistently finding ways to render them ineligible to receive medical care or access to a safe and fair education. *#sayhername*

So, I ask: Why? Why do we continue to perpetuate systems that value some individuals more than others, based on a dominant culture narrative that holds us all captive? Put simply, why does someone else's comfort level or understanding of my social identity and culture determine whether I am safe to enter a school classroom and have my identity respected in a way that fosters healthy human development, authentic relationships, self-confidence, and a general sense of physical safety? When I say "I," I mean anyone and everyone. I mean the child who has Brown or Black skin, the child who has same-sex parents, the child who is neuro-divergent, the child who says, "I'm not a boy, I'm a girl." I mean the families who have had to dedicate every opportunity to heal the multigenerational effects of genocide, exploitation, and erasure, working tirelessly to ensure that their children would know who they are, where they came from, how to speak their native language, and would have clean air and water.

When we speak of "inclusion and diversity," where is the line drawn? When we shy away from anything political, have you considered that my identity, my very being, has been politicized and fought for for decades, only to be given access when the right politicians are in office, or the right confluence of people are speaking up? I think often of how, if my grandparents had not risked their lives—to vote, to work, to be educated fairly—where would I be today? If not for the queer activists of the past—the drag queens and the people who came out of the closet even though they risked literally everything—would I be speaking to you today? Would I be your child's teacher?

In Waldorf education I have found much joy, purpose, and gratitude in the authentic presence of young children and for being given permission to witness the "becomingness" of the individuals in our care. At the same time, for a long time, I was reticent. I was young and I didn't see anyone who looked like me, or felt familiar in that unspoken way, whom I could aspire to be like. The explicit and implicit messages I received about the appropriate ways I was to act, dress, speak and think and celebrate, had overtones of european values and heteronormative ideals.

In her book *Braving the Wilderness*, Brene Brown (2017) states that fitting in is very different from true belonging. She says, "True belonging is the spiritual practice of believing in and belonging to yourself so deeply that you can share your most authentic self with the world and find sacredness in both being a part of something and standing alone in the wilderness. True belonging doesn't require you to change who you are, it requires you to BE who you are." As Waldorf teachers, I believe we need to inquire where we have been confusing inclusion with assimilation, or the expectation to fit into an ethos that was designed in a certain place and time. Being a Waldorf teacher has continuously called on me to stand authentically and wholly in front of classes of wide eyed, open eared young children who are asking me: Are you real and true?

An Introduction to Anti-Bias Education

Louise Derman-Sparks and her colleagues have written many books about antibias education in which they present four core principles: identity, diversity, justice, and action. These principles function like interlocking wheels, one turning the other. "Identity is in fact the foundation for the three other anti-bias core goals" (Derman-Sparks and Edwards 2010). If we have skipped this step, we will notice that despite all of our good intentions and wishing, things have changed but little.

Social identities relate to the significant group categorizations of the society in which people grow up and live, and that they share with many others. Social identities include but are not limited to gender, race, sexual orientation, ethnicity, cultural background, religion, and economic class. Personal identity is about how you see yourself as "different" from those around you. Hobbies, interests, personality traits, birth order, and other roles are personal identity traits. Social identities tell how you are like others—they connote similarity rather than difference. Some identities carry a different "privilege valence" or "oppression valence" than others. Not only does falling into a specific category give you a feeling of belonging and community, but it also implies the possibility of being seen as "one of those," which can lead to a sense of internalized stigmatization or shame for openly claiming membership in a particular group. *This* is the territory in which our biases lurk.

Parker Palmer, author of *The Courage to Teach* (2007) wrote, "We teach who we are." Waldorf teacher training starts with the inner work of the teacher, laying foundations for self-inquiry and reflection. Without active inquiry we are likely to be missing the implications of how our own social identities, biases, and settler-colonial mindsets are informing our daily choices and practices; for example, which order do we set the children in at the table or pair them with walking partners? What is informing parent night topics and articles, and what are we avoiding? Which stories and circles inspire and speak to us? And most importantly, what informs our behavioral expectations of the children? Back to my original inquiry: What is the source of our information about what it means to be respectful and respected?

Keelah

It's a warm day; the late summer heat still blankets our part of the world. I am wearing a crisp sundress, pressed to perfection, with a cardigan and my new school shoes from Buster Brown. My hair has been washed, worked through with an all-natural brand pomade and sprayed with Afro Sheen. It is sparkling. I'm wearing a special style, many small braids with brightly colored barrettes at the ends. I am nervous and clinging to my parents' hands. I am looking for the fold in my mother's skirt that I can roll into, coiling myself away from this scary day. My parents guide me around from behind them and introduce me to my teacher. I'm greeted with a warm smile and shepherded over to the "sailboat" that has run ashore on our playground. New friends approach me, and I settle in. It is 1976 and I'm a kindergartener at the Waldorf School of Garden City.

My teachers were kind and loving, and my childhood was lovely. In the wide openness of the young child, I consumed the soul nourishment of fairy tales, songs, poems, and verses, and drank in the imagery that filled my school day. My plate was so full, and my consumption so earnest, that I imagined myself in the meadows, castles, and forests of the fairy tales. What caused indigestion, however, was that every single princess, prince, king, and queen were white. All of the woodchoppers, the bakers, and the bootmakers were white. So too, were the mamas and papas and sisters and brothers and babies. All of the dolls, angels, fairies, wooden figurines, and paintings featured white folks, and every festival was from European tradition.

Rudolf Steiner said, "What the human being sees, what is poured into [their] environment, becomes a force in [them]. In accordance with it, the human being forms themself" (n.d.). When we are digesting properly it is an unconscious experience, unless there is some sort of dis-ease. And with the imitative gesture of the young child, I didn't notice that the food I was being served might not be so good for me—might not be intended for me at all; that this soul nourishment was not nourishing my soul; that it might not be enough to grow on. But I wasn't conscious, nor should I have been. I struggled, leaning, stretching toward an ideal that was both implicit and explicit. The ideal of whiteness. My parents noticed, bless them. They made certain that the stories, songs, and images in our home reflected the beautiful joy of being Black to their daughter. They also told me stories that weren't beautiful. I remember walking into a room where my grandmother was ironing and noticed that she was crying. When I asked why, she told me that she was all right, just thinking about her husband.

You see, my grandfather was a mechanic and a musician. He and three friends formed a gospel a cappella group called the Humble Jubilee quartet and they toured the region performing at different churches and at summer revivals. One day, after working at the autobody shop, my grandfather was walking home. He was struck by a car and dragged to his death by the driver, a young white man. The driver fled the scene, and later was apprehended when the car was discovered in his backyard. He was never charged or prosecuted, nor were there any amends made. My grandmother was left a widow with two young children, my mom and uncle left without a father.

Years passed, and when I was an adolescent in the throes of identity development, I began to write myself into the Waldorf curriculum. In every book report, biography, or special project that I was assigned, I chose to make a Black person's story and accomplishments the topic. Oftentimes, I had to make a special request for approval of my selected subject, because BIPOC names were not included on the recommended list. As a high school student I was very aware of the fact that a duality had emerged between my school life and my home life. At home, my bookshelves were lined with stories of dynamic, interesting, smart, adventurous Black and Brown people.

In my church youth group and neighborhood, my experience as a Black young woman in the United States was affirmed, recognized and supported.

And that, dear colleagues—that's what was missing in my thirteen years as a Waldorf student. I was loved, yes, but I was not seen. The fact that I existed in a society that was racist, hostile, and dangerous, simply because of the skin I was blessed with, was ignored.

An Introduction to Racial Identity Development

Biography is a path, a way in, an opportunity to reflect, to see anew, to recognize, to unearth, to reveal that which may have been hidden or forgotten. It is a remembering, a re-member-ing—the many parts of ourselves. As Meggan brought us all along a journey of naming and claiming our identities, we begin to see ourselves with more clarity, more authenticity, and more complexity. Our stories are our own, and they reflect our unique experience as human beings living on this earth. But there is a common thread that we share, a thread to a blanket that none of us created; but yet, we are heirs and victims, we are repairing patches, we are tearing it apart, we are beneficiaries, we are the dispossessed, but not a one of us is spared its weight.

It is the blanket of racism.

It appears to warm some, smother others, protect many, and extinguish the light of most. But colleagues, racism is insidious, and it suffocates us all. Racism has told us the lie that some are valued above others, that some are deserving of beauty, of childhood, safety, protection, food and shelter, love and freedom. Racism coaxes us to feel as if it is just and justified. Racism causes us to go against our own interests and create, support, and defend complex systems that benefit some at the harm and detriment of others. Racism strips us of our humanity and stunts our evolution, it halts our growth and undermines our development. And it does its job with brilliant precision, such that it lulls some of us to sleep, thinking that all is well, I am well, this is normal.

And here I am, here we are, calling for that blanket to be thrown off, examined, assessed, and deemed futile in the future we seek to create, in the future our children deserve, and the future that love demands. Rudolf Steiner encouraged us to be awake in our times and that awakening requires us to galvanize great courage.

Each one of us has been racialized, has been labeled, sorted, and assigned value based simply on the skin we are in, the curl of our hair, and the width of our noses. We live in racialized societies where everyone is assigned a racial identity whether they are aware of it or not. We define racial identity as being externally imposed: "How do others perceive me?" And racial identity is also internally constructed: "How do I identify myself?" And even though we did not ask for it, we are all navigating a society built upon it. Race matters, our racial identity matters, and it matters a lot. And it means something different to each one of us.

There is a way in, a sensing, a way of knowing ourselves that remains unexamined. An opening to assess how all of the stories we have been told about the other—all of the messages, subtle judgements, jokes, and taunts that live in our subconscious and in our bodies—have shaped us.

Racial identity development theory represents a body of work created by Dr. William Cross and Dr. Janet Helms, and is expanded upon by Dr. Beverly Daniel Tatum. It offers us tools to make sense of our experiences, what we see, think, and feel about race. We all come to the table shaped by our families, neighborhoods, communities, and education. And all of those messages that we heard loud and clear, as well as the quieter, subtler messages that we just inhaled and ingested—all of them inform who we are and how we see ourselves in the world. And it is not until we start to unearth and understand how racism has impacted and shaped our lives as adults that we can begin to meet the children in our care as our most authentic selves. When we are together again, we will utilize the gifts of our own biographies to find ourselves on the continuum of racial identity development as we strive to be ever finer representations of the human being on behalf of the children in our care.

We all have a story. We have all, somehow, in small or bigger ways, been impacted by race or racism. Think back to the earliest time you realized you had a racial identity. Describe as much as you can about that experience. What did this experience teach you about your own race?

Explore: Story Telling

Compiled by M. Gill for Alma Partners

- WHY?
- What gives us "permission" to tell stories from outside our own culture?
- How are you engaging in learning?
- What happens when we omit certain stories from our repertoire?
- How do we tell stories: books, plays, oral telling, puppetry, Heritage Months or Celebrations
- What do you hope the children will receive from the story?

Joaquin

Teaching has been my passion for more than seventeen years. I have been a teacher and educator in some capacity since the summer of 2005, when I received my training as a middle-years instructor through Teach For America (TFA). I taught in North Philadelphia, working primarily with youth from Puerto Rico, the Dominican Republic, and Cuba. In this environment, it quickly became evident to me that my preconceived notions of working with students were not the most effective means for instruction. In my thinking, I would be lecturing to students who would be 100 percent attentive, and my voice and presence would be enough to guide them. These assumptions were largely misplaced. Three grueling months of little sleep, trying to cope with students' behavioral issues, and overdependence on veteran teachers on my floor caused me to completely rethink my strategy for working with students. By the end of my first year of teaching, the only thing I was sure of was the need to change. I rethought all of my assumptions, all of my TFA training, and decided I needed a new approach.

That summer, I completely recreated all of my classroom systems. Every aspect of my teaching activity was transformed, starting with restructuring the rules and procedures in my class. I centered talking and structured conversation circles in my classes, to give my students opportunities to discuss and build community. I abandoned the vast majority of the scripted curriculum assigned for the class and I incorporated hip-hop, social media, and other text structures to meet classroom objectives. I found techniques like these to be more engaging for students and more supportive of their success. I took these approaches with me to my next adventure, in my home state of Arizona.

After moving back to Arizona in the summer of 2007, I began to work with elementary and middle school students from the tribal community where I grew up. Here, I continued to use the various learning techniques I had developed in Philadelphia. Working as a tutor for the Native American Studies program, I used activities such as coordination games to teach chess and guitar, and taught seventh graders probability using blackjack. I enrolled as a master's degree student in the Language, Reading and Culture program at the

University of Arizona. After earning my MA, the opportunity for me to work with an entirely new population of students emerged, as I began work as a teaching assistant and adjunct faculty member. In these roles, I continued my use of alternative learning methods, now blended with the critical perspectives of history, culture, and theory I had learned.

In 2011, I began my doctoral program in Language, Reading and Culture. I continued to explore components of critical pedagogy, and I also looked to expand my understanding of new paradigms for instructing students. I was excited, but still felt hollow. The sense of something missing was still present. I loved my courses, but still felt I had a need not being met. A conversation with a mentor, who was also an educator, directed my attention to Waldorf education. The conversation was rather cryptic though: he simply mentioned that I might look into Waldorf schools as an alternative, and said nothing more.

I began with exploring the possibility of attending a Waldorf teacher training session or education seminar, hoping to become better acquainted with the practices of the schools. I learned about Rudolf Steiner College (RSC) in Fair Oaks, California and I discovered several training programs at RSC, including the Public School Institute (PSI), which provided training to public school teachers in Waldorf methods through an immersion program. I inquired into the program, describing my interests in Waldorf education as a scholar, a teacher, and educator concerned with outcomes for Native American students. After a number of conversations, I was surprised and honored to discover that the administrators of the PSI, Arlene Monks and Sandra Gill, had nominated me to receive funding from a fellowship program that supported Native American teachers to attend the PSI, all expenses paid. They secured funding for me, and for two weeks in July of 2013, I was a student at RSC.

Upon my return from RSC, I began to consider the possibility of utilizing Waldorf-inspired methods in my own practice. I began to formulate the ways they might be implemented into my community college and university classrooms. Thus began the development of my Waldorf-inspired courses at Pima College, courses I taught at the University of Arizona, and eventually to my career as a professor of education.

An Introduction to Cultural Appropriation, Appreciation, and Assimilation

My goal during these sessions is to help us in developing our understanding of culture, cultural appropriation, and cultural appreciation. And I want to frame this thinking through the work of one of my heroes, Dr. Martin Luther King Jr., and use two of his conceptions: of love and power. Dr. King wrote that "Power without love is reckless and abusive . . . love without power is sentimental and anemic" (King [1968] 1994, 38). Scholar and social change advocate Adam Kahane (2009), analyzing Dr. King, goes on to discuss how love with power is generative; it allows for relationship and community and a "drive toward the unity of the separated" which does not force conformity or assimilation. Power with love is generative, "power to"; it allows for the loving support of all to engage the intrinsic drive to "realize itself, with greater intensity and extensity." Thus, we have these two powers, and two loves, to consider: generative and degenerative power, and generative and degenerative love.

As an educator committed to social justice, anti-racism and anti-oppression, the ideas relating our power and our love guide my actions and my questions. I think about what an "education for the future" means, in the light of our diverse world. I consider that social change is happening—it's a fact of life—and what this means for how we engage teaching and learning. And I think about all of the ways that I impact social change: and whether this is for greater and greater freedom, or old practices that can oppress and hurt. We need to rethink our work of diversity—which is a practice often informed by anemic love. We need to develop and share our power—our privileges—to support all people to self-realize and self-actualize. Only then can we all be our most complete selves. Then diversity can actually be acknowledged and appreciated, and inclusion effectively practiced.

What does this mean for the questions of culture, appropriation, and appreciation? It means that our understanding of culture—the patterns of shared basic assumptions, behaviors, and experiences within a group of people by which they learn and are taught—must be understood through the lens of history, survivance, and an internal logic that makes it work. It means we have to understand how our degenerative power has erased cultures, and how our degenerative love attempts to bring cultures into our classrooms without full respect and understanding for what we are bringing, and why. It means that our degenerative power and degenerative love create conditions of cultural appropriation, which is the taking of intellectual property, traditional knowledge, cultural expressions, or artifacts from someone else's culture—including dance, dress, music, language, folklore, cuisine, traditional medicine, religious symbols—without permission.

What, on the other hand, is a vision of cultural appreciation? What is the vision and practice of sharing about cultures—usually not our own—with respect, with equity, with justice, and with accuracy in mind? We can also ask: what power—or privilege, to say this another way—are we enacting? Is our power generative, or "power to," when we carefully curate what we bring in? Is our power generative when we embrace and face the reality of history, even if it is scary or uncomfortable? And we can ask: what kind of love are we enacting? Is it the generative love that builds relationships with those in our specific place? Is it a generative love that seeks to practice humility? How are we using our power and our love, my friends?

References

Brown, Brene. 2017. *Braving the Wilderness: The Quest for True Belonging and the Courage to Stand Alone.* New York: Random House.

Derman-Sparks, Louise, and Julie Olsen Edwards. 2010. *Anti-Bias Education for Young Children and Ourselves.* Washington, DC: National Association for the Education of Young Children.

Kahane, Adam. Dec. 9, 2009. "An Introduction to *Power and Love: A Theory and Practice of Social Change.*" Reos Partners. https://reospartners.com/an-introduction-to-power-and-love-a-theory-and-practice-of-social-change/.

King, Martin Luther, Jr. (1968) 1994. *Where Do We Go from Here: Chaos or Community?* Boston: Beacon Press. https://www.uni-five.com/upload/doc/82818file.pdf.

Palmer, Parker. 2007. *The Courage to Teach: Exploring the Inner Landscape of a Teacher's Life*. 10th Anniversary Edition. Hoboken, NJ: Jossey-Bass.

Steiner, Rudolf (attributed). N.d. "What the human being sees . . ." See, e.g., Brainy Quote. https://www.brainyquote.com/quotes/rudolf_steiner_777960.

Additional Resources

#SayTheirNames. https://sayevery.name/

Landback.org.

Sensing Ourselves: Uncovering our Identity Through the Lens of Biography

Meggan: On Antibias Education

As we digest this work, we encounter some things that may be painful—
I have loved, but I have not seen.
I have heard, but I have not listened.
I have looked, but through eyes that were trained on a certain view.
I have tried to change, but it feels beyond my reach.

You may be asking:
How can I see beyond my own field of vision?
How can I change my perspective if it's all I know?
How is what I'm not seeing impacting the children in my care?

To understand antibias work, we can begin by understanding the nature of bias. Jennifer Eberhardt, in her book *Biased: Uncovering the Hidden Prejudice That Shapes What We See, Think, and Do* (2019), says "Implicit bias is a kind of distorting lens that's a product of both the architecture of our brains and the disparities in our society." Bias is a natural thing to admit when it's considered in terms of innocuous partiality; for instance, I am partial, or biased, toward live music. However, bias is also present in our relationships to people and social groups. It is heavily influenced by pervasive presentations of stereotypes, upheld by systems of power, economy, and imbalanced cultural representation. And the impact of it starts very young.

I know that as a parent and an early childhood teacher I can recount many instances where I have heard and witnessed exchanges from children as young as two years old who pronounce judgements, announce "facts," and ask questions about differences in other people that can feel confounding or embarrassing.

And then begins internal cascade:

Where did they learn that? Should I say something? What should I say? They didn't mean any harm; will saying something make it worse?

Who is to blame? Is it the parents? Is it other people's children? Is it just the media? Or could it be something less tangible, but more pervasive-dominant culture.

In the meantime, the children are watching, as silence, physical discomfort, or an undigested series of words spill out, trying to mask the truth of the pain. Bias seeps into every aspect of our culture, our family norms, and schooling. The stories we are told from a young age are told from one perspective, even if they are multicultural—the teller picks from within their own biases. The people in our neighborhoods and schools reflect shared economy and access, and generally include certain behavioral norms.

So, what can we do?

According to Jennifer Eberhardt (2019), one of the easiest things we can do is to create friction. In our minds, "friction" is typically something we want to avoid—so I want to invite you to help me collectively reframe this word. A picture I like to use is of my bicycle brake: I squeeze the handle and the brake pad applies friction on the wheel that's steadily in motion, while my eyes are focused ahead and my body is following. It's my mind that tells me to slow down, assess, make choices.

In order to wake up the unconscious mind from its comfy slumber of assumptions while things move forward, we use what we call mindfulness tools. Mindfulness provides a way for us to slow down, interrupt and counter the narrative, pause, reflect, observe, and change our course. Adding friction can look like letting go of thinking that we know the "right way," questioning our assumptions about the conditions we've created, and importantly, notice what we are avoiding. What does it look like when I try a different way? What is the effect if I tell the story to reflect another perspective or add dimension to a one-sided view? For instance, consider this: How would it be, for you personally, if the king and queen as a married pair were presented as different, unusual, and whispered about, and the norm were only noble queens and sisters who got along? Sisters who didn't quarrel or compete, but cooperated and shared—this would be a mirror for me. There would be no "kingdoms" in stories reflecting my experience, because for my community land ownership didn't exist. This would reflect Indigenous truths.

How would it be for you to let go of the idea of binary genders altogether and to focus instead on the expansive qualities of the characters? Could this save a child's life?

How would it be, for you, if white-bodied people were historically marginalized, subservient, and added to stories as a gesture, or as sidekicks, but not as the benevolent masters and keepers of the gold? How would it be to consider that all the gold in the stories we've been telling was stolen from the Indigenous peoples, along with their homelands?

Meditation:

Another way in which we can add friction is through meditation. Studies have shown that practicing loving-kindness (in Buddhism, the Metta) can increase compassion and decrease implicit bias. This version can be found in *The Inner Work of Racial Justice*, by Rhonda Magee (2021, 274)

Begin by centering yourself in space and place, connecting with your breath. Call to your mind's eye:

- A benevolent being, someone from whom you've received or experienced unconditional love, care, nurturing, or support
- Your self, at any age or time of yourself that you wish to connect with
- Someone you know, but not well—an acquaintance; or someone with whom you face challenges or difficulties.

To each, with time and breath in between, repeat these wishes:

May you be filled with loving-kindness.
May you be well, in body and in mind.
May you be safe from inner and outer dangers.
May you be truly happy and free.

Keelah: Racial Identity Development

When we were last together in our conference in 2022, "Toward a Kinder More Compassionate Society, Black Lives Matter in Waldorf Early Childhood Programs," we were collectively in the midst of a whirlwind. The macrocosm of our society entered into the microcosm of our peach-blossom, Lazured rooms. In many of our schools, early childhood teachers were leading the charge—we were on fire! We attended webinars, we brought what we were learning, questioning, and unearthing to our section meetings, we held class meetings and spoke to our parents about representation and cultural appreciation; anti-racist work lived in our collegial work and conversation and study. And questions emerged:

- Are the children too young to notice skin color?
- Am I supposed to tell the parents what has changed in the classroom?
- What if my colleagues don't agree with the changes I've made?
- What if I don't agree with the lack of change in my colleagues' classroom?

- And what if I don't think my colleagues should have changed anything at all?
- What about all the energy we put into being practitioners who work with implicit learning?
- If we are explicit, are we still Waldorf early childhood educators?

And those questions that we hold deep inside ourselves ripple outwards, and we see them playing out on the world stage. And we feel the tension, the push and pull, the reckoning of systemic racism, and the need to act, and the persistent gnawing—or lulling—feeling that it is all too much. Words like compassion fatigue, polarization, and divisiveness enter in..

We awaken and question whether the pressure to recognize racism and anti-racism is really divisive, or is it just that the burden has only been on the backs of Black, Indigenous, and people of color? And that sends us back into the work, back into the exploration, the conversation, the meditation, and the action.

In my work I have come across an invaluable tool that offers us all an entry point into a deeper sensing and knowing of ourselves as racialized beings. And from that place of authentic self-awareness, that knowing can radiate outward and offer us wisdom to sense our children.

I ask for blessings on our journey together.

When we engage in work like this, it is tough. We start to examine things that may have been asleep or dormant for a very long time. As we work, tune into your bodies. Sense where tension arises and acknowledge it, be curious about it. Jot a note down for later inquiry. Processing with a trusted friend who is also on this journey can prove supportive and helpful.

And what is vital? Breathing.

When we experience the pangs and "ahas," we can often inhale sharply and forget to exhale. Breathe deeply, dear colleagues, breathe deeply. Sense what is bubbling up for us right now.

So as a point of clarity, the conversation that we are having revolves exclusively around race and racism. The vast and beautiful umbrella of social identities including gender, ability, gender expression, sexuality, age, religion, and class find numerous points of intersection, but right now we are holding a narrow focus on race and racial identity.

As we begin to delve into the racial identity models, I am offering wisdom from deep thinkers who expand the definition of race. The scientific consensus is that race has no biological basis—we are all one race, the human race. But this definition and consensus is incomplete. The definition misses the complexity of the impact of race on lived experiences. It is important to acknowledge race is a social fabrication, created to classify people on the arbitrary basis of skin color (phenotype) and other physical features. And, although race has no genetic or scientific basis, the concept of race is important and consequential. Societies use race to establish and justify systems of power, privilege, disenfranchisement, and oppression. TaNahesi Coates (2014) informs us that "It is important to remember that American racism is a thing that was done, and a world where American racism is beaten back is not a world of 'racial diversity' but a world without such terminology. Perhaps we can never actually get to that World. Perhaps we are just too far gone. But we should never forget that this world was 'made.' Whiteness and [B]lackness are not a fact of providence, but of policy—of slave codes, black codes, Jim Crow, redlining, GI Bills, housing covenants, New Deals, and mass incarcerations."

And as our focus becomes ever sharper, we are examining these concepts as they appear and emerge.

In the groundbreaking California Newsreel documentary, *RACE: The Power of an Illusion* (2003a), the following ten-point statement sheds light on the unique, intentionally created bondage of race in the United States.

Ten Things Everyone Should Know About Race

(California Newsreel 2003b)

Our eyes tell us that people look different. No one has trouble distinguishing a Czech from a Chinese, but what do those differences mean? Are they biological? Has race always been with us? How does race affect people today? There's less—and more—to race than meets the eye:

1. Race is a modern idea. Ancient societies, like the Greeks, did not divide people according to physical distinctions, but according to religion, status, class, even language. The English language didn't even have the word "race" until it turns up in 1508 in a poem by William Dunbar referring to a line of kings.

2. Race has no genetic basis. Not one characteristic, trait or even one gene distinguishes all the members of one so-called race from all the members of another so-called race.

3. Human subspecies don't exist. Unlike many animals, modern humans simply haven't been around long enough or isolated enough to evolve into separate subspecies or races. Despite surface appearances, we are one of the most similar of all species.

4. Skin color really is only skin deep. Most traits are inherited independently from one another. The genes influencing skin color have nothing to do with the genes influencing hair form, eye shape, blood type, musical talent, athletic ability or forms of intelligence. Knowing someone's skin color doesn't necessarily tell you anything else about him or her.

5. Most variation is within, not between, "races." Of the small amount of total human variation, 85% exists within any local population, be they Italians, Kurds, Koreans or Cherokees. About 94% can be found within any continent. That means two random Koreans may be as genetically different as a Korean and an Italian.

6. Slavery predates race. Throughout much of human history, societies have enslaved others, often as a result of conquest or war, even debt, but

not because of physical characteristics or a belief in natural inferiority. Due to a unique set of historical circumstances, ours was the first slave system where all the slaves shared similar physical characteristics.

7. Race and freedom evolved together. The U.S. was founded on the radical new principle that "All men are created equal." But our early economy was based largely on slavery. How could this anomaly be rationalized? The new idea of race helped explain why some people could be denied the rights and freedoms that others took for granted.

8. Race justified social inequalities as natural. As the race idea evolved, white superiority became "common sense" in America. It justified not only slavery but also the extermination of [Native Americans], exclusion [and internment] of Asian immigrants, and the taking of Mexican lands by a nation that professed a belief in democracy. Racial practices were institutionalized within American government, laws, and society.

9. Race isn't biological, but racism is still real. Race is a powerful social idea that gives people different access to opportunities and resources. Our government and social institutions have created advantages that disproportionately channel wealth, power, and resources to white people. This affects everyone, whether we are aware of it or not.

10. Colorblindness will not end racism. Pretending race doesn't exist is not the same as creating equality. Race is more than stereotypes and individual prejudice. To combat racism, we need to identify and remedy social policies and institutional practices that advantage some groups at the expense of others.

> *The world got along without race for the overwhelming majority of its history. The U.S. has never been without it.*
>
> *—Smithsonian Library of the African American, quoting David R. Roediger (2010)*

How Racial Identity Is Formed

When we talk about racial identity formation, Dr. Beverly Tatum, in her groundbreaking book *Why Are All the Black Kids Sitting Together in the Cafeteria?*, shares that racial identity "Refers to the process of defining for oneself the personal significance and social meaning of belonging to a particular racial group." She goes on to state, "The language we use to categorize one another racially is imperfect. These categories are still evolving . . . The original creation of racial categories was in the service of oppression. Some may argue that to continue to use them is to continue that oppression." I share her respect for that argument. Yet, she states, "it is difficult to talk about what is essentially a flawed and problematic social construct without using language that is itself problematic. We have to be able to talk about it in order to change it."

Racial identity development is a lifelong process, in constant movement. We may reach one phase only to go back to another. We may move through several quickly or be stuck in one. During this process, people move between a desire to "fit in" to dominant norms, to a questioning of one's own identity and that of others. It is a continuous process: a process of defining and redefining ourselves. There are multiple models. There may be stages that align with your personal experience, and there may be stages that do not. We all have a story. We have all, somehow, in small or large ways, been impacted by race or racism.

The first model that I will introduce was developed by Dr. William Cross (1991). Initially it was titled "People of Color"; many now extend it to encompass BIPOC experience. New terms are emerging daily, and we are steadily expanding our vocabulary.

As we begin, please hold in your hearts families, students, and colleagues of color. See their faces; surround them with your warmth and love. See them thriving in our schools, see them arriving in their fullness.

I must begin by acknowledging that work in this field is still developing and there is a great need for models that share insight to the experience of MENA identities (Middle Eastern / North African). Some of the countries included in MENA are Algeria, Bahrain, Egypt, Iran, Iraq,

Israel, Jordan, Kuwait, Lebanon, Libya, Morocco, Oman, Qatar, Saudi Arabia, Syria, Tunisia, United Arab Emirates, and Yemen. Models including Asian Pacific Americans and Asian Pacific Islander (APA/API) identities and nations such as Indonesia, Samoa, India, Pakistan, Bangladesh, Sri Lanka, Nepal, Bhutan, Japan, China, Taiwan, Korea, Indonesia, Vietnam, Laos, Cambodia, the Philippines, Samoa, Fiji, and Guam are also needed.

Racial Identity Development

(Tatum 2017, citing Cross 1991)

People of Color:

Pre-encounter: The individual seeks to assimilate and be accepted by whites, and actively or passively distances themself from other persons of their own race. This de-emphasis on one's racial-group membership may allow the individual to think that race has not been or will not be a relevant factor in one's own achievement.

Encounter: Movement into the Encounter phases is typically precipitated by an event or series of events that forces the individual to acknowledge the impact of racism in one's life. Faced with the reality that they cannot truly be white, the individual is forced to focus on their identity as a member of a group targeted by racism. (Author's note: I think about when I learned of my grandfather's murder, related above in "Sensing Each One.")

Immersion/Emersion: This stage is characterized by the simultaneous desire to surround oneself with visible symbols of one's racial identity and active avoidance of symbols of whiteness. Individuals in this stage actively seek out opportunities to explore aspects of their own history and culture with the support of peers from their own racial background. (Author's note: I think about when I started AFRICA in my basement.)

Internalization: In this stage, secure in one's own sense of racial identity, there is less need to assert the "Blacker than thou" or similar attitudes often characteristic of the prior stage. One's attitudes favoring one's own racial identity become more expansive, open, and less defensive. The individual who has internalized their racial identity is willing to establish meaningful relationships with whites who acknowledge and are respectful of their self-definition. The individual is also ready to build coalitions with members of other oppressed groups

Internalization-Commitment: Those in this last stage have found ways to translate their personal sense of race into a plan of action or general sense of commitment to the concerns of their own race as a group. This is sustained over time. Their race becomes the point of departure for discovering the universe of ideas, cultures, and experiences beyond their own race, in place of mistaking their race as the universe itself. This can be seen as a goal of Waldorf education; how are we laying the groundwork for this?

Encounters with race and racism will continue. Sometimes one will return to the immersion/emersion stage (I need to connect with my group) or perhaps to the internalization stage (I need to reconnect with my coalition). After leaving the pre-encounter stage, there is never a return. Once you are aware of racism, there is never a "forgetting" or going back. This is a "fall from Eden" experience.

The next model I will introduce is the Biracial Identity model, developed by Dr. Carlos Poston (1990). As we begin, please hold in your hearts families, students, and colleagues who are biracial. See their faces, surround them with your warmth and love. See them thriving in Waldorf schools. See them arriving in their fullness.

Biracial Identity Development

(Poston 1990)

Personal Identity: The individual experiences a sense of self unrelated to ethnic grouping; typically, this stage occurs during childhood.

Choice Of Group: as a result of multiple factors, individuals feel pressured to choose one racial or ethnic group identity over another. Society says "I am," and many people are plagued with questions of "What are you?" Where are we intentionally offering images that support our children?

Categorization: The individual may make choices influenced by the status of the racial group. Racial groups exist in this society in a hierarchy that involves parental influence, cultural knowledge, or appearance. Biracial individuals are defined by the way they are "seen" or by what society assumes them to be. Where are we making assumptions?

Enmeshment/Denial: The individual may experience guilt and confusion about choosing an identity that isn't fully expressive of all their cultural influences; the individual can feel as if they are denying a part of themselves. There can be a denial of differences between the racial groupings; the individual may choose to explore the identities that were not chosen in the choice of group and categorization stages.

Appreciation: of multiple identities. All of the identities are held with regard.

Integration: A tapestry is woven together from the many threads and a sense of wholeness emerges through the integration of multiple identities. How do we stand in support?

The final model that I will introduce includes six stages for white identity development. It was created by Dr. Janet Helms (1990). As we begin, please hold in your hearts families, students, and colleagues who are white. Imagine their faces, surround them with warmth and love. See them experiencing a decentering of whiteness and a re-centering of a global appreciation; see them meeting truth; see them participating and thriving in equitable, just spaces.

Six Stages for White Identity Development

(Helms 1990)

Contact: A lack of awareness of cultural and institutional racism, and of one's own white privilege. This stage often includes naive curiosity about or fear of people of color, based on stereotypes learned from friends, family, or the media. Those whose lives are structured so as to limit their interaction with people of color, as well as their awareness of racial issues, may remain at this stage indefinitely. How are we engaged as "social justice doulas"; how are we supporting growth in each other, in our colleagues? Are our institutions stuck in this stage?

Disintegration: Increased interaction with people of color or new information about racism may lead to a new understanding, which marks the beginning of this stage. In this stage, the bliss of ignorance or lack of awareness is replaced by the discomfort of guilt, shame, and sometimes anger at the recognition of one's own advantage in being white and the acknowledgement of the role of whites in maintaining a racist system. Attempts to reduce discomfort may include denial or attempts to change significant others' attitudes toward people of color. Societal pressure to accept the status quo may lead the individual from the disintegration stage to the reintegration stage. How are colleagues supported in your school as they move through this stage?

Reintegration: At this point the desire to be accepted by one's own racial group, in which the overt or covert belief in white superiority is so prevalent, may lead to a reshaping of the person's belief system to be more congruent with attitudes accepting of racism. The guilt and anxiety may be redirected as fear and anger directed toward people of color who are now blamed as the source of discomfort. It is easy for whites to become stuck at this stage of development, particularly if avoidance of people of color is possible. How are we creating opportunities for movement through the calcifying aspect of this stage?

Pseudo-Independent: Seeking information about people of color often marks the onset of this stage. The individual is abandoning beliefs in white superiority, but may still behave in ways that unintentionally perpetuate the system. Looking to those targeted by racism to help them understand, the white person often tries to disavow their own whiteness through active affiliation with persons of color. The individual experiences a sense of alienation from other whites who have not yet begun to examine their own racism, yet may also experience rejection from persons of color who are suspicious of his or her motives. Persons of color moving from the encounter to immersion stages of their own racial identity development may be particularly unreceptive to a white person's attempts to connect with them.

Immersion/Emersion: Uncomfortable with their own whiteness, yet unable to be truly anything else, the individual may begin searching for a new, more comfortable way to be white in this stage. Learning about whites who have been antiracist allies to people of color is an important part of this process. Whites find it helpful to know that others have experienced similar feelings and have found ways to resist the racism in their environments, and they are provided with important models for change. Are we creating white affinity spaces of support and development?

Autonomy: The internalization of a newly defined sense of self as white is the primary task of this stage. The positive feelings associated with this redefinition energize the person's efforts to confront racism and oppression in daily life. Alliances with people of color can be more easily forged in this stage because the person's anti-racist behaviors and attitudes will be more consistently expressed.

When we engage in racial identity development self-work like this, whether we are BIPOC or white, we move the needle. We stretch, we evolve, and become ever finer representations of the human being for our students. And here is where we can take another step forward. There is urgency to this work, because woven into the fabric of being a Waldorf early childhood teacher is our commitment to knowing the children before us. If we are to truly know the whole child, we must also explore and become conversant with how their racial identity is shifting and evolving in our classrooms each and every day. Our intention is to know the students before us. But I propose that there is something missing in that "knowing" if we are not awake to the racialized society that we live in and the fact that our children exist in it right along with us. Dr. Tatum talks about a racist smog—no one told us to put on a mask for that pandemic. Where our children exist in the ebb and flow of these models influences what we bring to them and how we bring it, and how they receive it.

And if we truly engage in this work, holding it in the same regard to which we hold the children in our sleep and meditative life, awakening to their experiences of being racialized beings in this society, we receive a rare gift. We move closer to becoming the educators that our children deserve as we continue to remove obstacles on the path.

Joaquin: On Cultural Appropriation, Appreciation, and Assimilation

My goal during these sessions is to help us in developing our understanding of cultural appreciation and cultural appropriation, and in order to do that we need to begin with an understanding of culture. Culture encompasses so many different aspects of our life are experience and the ways we make sense of the world. It is important to start here in order to be able to have a better understanding of what exactly it means when someone says, "This is cultural appropriation" or "That is cultural appreciation."

So, let's begin by thinking about cultural awareness and how we think about cultures. We often think about some of the surface-level aspects of culture, the things that are easily accessible and easily seen as being differences. And so, oftentimes when we focus on culture, we can ignore or miss some of its more fundamental pieces because it is easier for us to access and understand what is on the surface. And so, because we often focus on the surface, and often miss the lower levels, we misinterpret or misunderstand aspects of culture in different ways. One way is in claims of universalism, and a belief that in essence all people are the same or identical, with some small differences. This, however, is not an accurate assessment, given that all groups of people have distinct characteristics and practices that make them unique human beings. Added to this is the challenge of an assumption that cultures are the same; we are interpreting them using our own cultural lenses, giving hyper-attention to similarities, and downplaying differences.

In education, we often focus on the surface levels of culture and this can be seen in lessons or content that explores the surface-level differences of communities: stories, dance, dress or outfit, food, and other elements that are easily visible. Oftentimes this is the safest level for us to engage in, but at the same time it requires less awareness and knowledge on our part. In some ways the surface level of culture is the least complex because it is the one that is most easily accessible. However, a deeper examination of culture points to multiple concepts and themes which are much harder to understand and much more complicated to integrate in a space like a classroom—aspects of culture like different conceptions of physical proximity and comfort, or different perceptions of tone of voice and meaning, to name just two.

Knowledge and understanding are central to bringing diverse cultural experiences into the classroom. We cannot only focus on the surface level, but we must be willing to explore further down. This is particularly true if we are teachers who represent dominant social identities examining the experiences of cultures that have been minoritized or oppressed. It is always helpful to remember a few crucial concepts when exploring culture for its inclusion in the classroom:

- All aspects of culture, even those aspects that we disagree with, don't like, or don't understand, have a logic that makes them function.
- We have to remember that all aspects of culture require knowledgeable carriers. Knowledge keepers have often suffered—and continue to suffer—for carrying the cultural knowledge they have.
- It's important to remember that all aspects of culture inform each other. Another way to say this is that every experience of culture, whether it's food, psychology, music, or ways of knowing the world, are interrelated to each other.

With this as a starting point, we can begin to explore why the topic of cultural appropriation is such an important as well as sensitive topic to consider. The scholar Maisha Z. Johnson (2017) defines cultural appropriation as any taking from a marginalized group usually without respect for or knowledge of their culture. This definition should immediately cause us to consider some key concepts: history, power, and complexity. In thinking about cultures, we have to think about the history of the treatment of different peoples, such as Black, Indigenous and people of color, who have unique histories in relation to the United States. This history includes enslavement, genocide, forced removal, and kidnapping. This history must be considered when planning to engage these communities in the classroom. Power must also be considered—how power has been used historically and in contemporary situations to demonstrate dominance and control. In this way, decisions we make about cultural artifacts, stories, or histories being brought into the classroom should be considered carefully with relation to power. Whose identity is considered to have power and decision-making capability? And what does that mean for including or excluding others? Finally, we must attend to the complexity of cultures. This means that we must attend to the rich diversity within communities as well as the constantly changing nature of culture. Teachers often ask about the inclusion of Indigenous peoples' stories in their classroom content, which frequently means the inclusion of stories which frame Indigenous peoples as historical relics. Little or no attention is given to the contemporary expressions of Indigenous personhood, and this can communicate to young people that "real" Indigenous people are in the past.

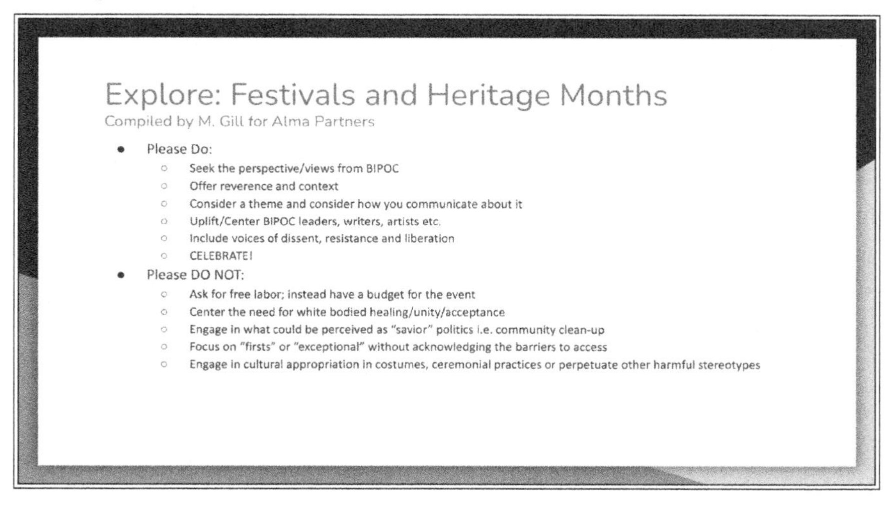

A crucial concern for many teachers is clear definitions around cultural appropriation and how this is different from forms of cultural violence. The two are interrelated but different. Cultural appropriation often takes the form of sharing, repackaging, or communicating information without an awareness of the proper protocols, practices, or context for where those cultural expressions came from. This can often mean teachers or educators sharing stories without the context of where they came from or why they are important. This can also mean the sharing of cultural elements without proper credit, acknowledgment, or compensation to the creator.

Cultural violence, on the other hand, is a far more problematic practice and often involves the communication of harmful stereotypes and prejudices with no move to redress those harms. Examples of cultural violence related to cultural appropriation often include school mascots depicting Indigenous people, or the example of a California schoolteacher who used a construction paper headdress and stereotypical "Indian" war chants to teach a math lesson. These examples are egregious versions; but smaller acts of cultural appropriation should not be ignored as being less problematic or traumatizing.

Some common practices of cultural appropriation in school settings include monetizing or profiting off of another person's culture without appropriate compensation. Another form occurs when a member of a community practicing their culture is seen as deviant or problematic, but the same practice is seen as interesting or creative when practiced by someone of dominant culture. For example, certain hairstyles or artistic expressions, when practiced by African American youth, are seen as negative, while white youth engaging the same practices are seen as interesting or creative. Another form is the careful selection of elements of culture to share what is seen as positive inclusion, but the selection is problematic because it only represents carefully curated examples of diverse communities. This curation can often uphold certain people's visions of power and privilege, as well as framing certain members of diverse communities as being the "true" representations. For Indigenous people this often comes in the form of a hyper-focus on spirituality, or connection to the natural world, without sharing other aspects such as contemporary authors, artists, or political activists. In African American communities this is often seen as the focus on peaceful agitators such as Dr. Martin Luther King Jr. without attending to other expressions of African American culture. Cherry-picking like this often upholds biases and stereotypes because they do not challenge status-quo visions and interpretations of reality.

To move toward appreciation, we have to begin to investigate an alternative way of being with people. This includes focusing on healing wounds and trauma and working to prevent future wounds and trauma. As we move away from cultural appropriation practices and cultural violence we must begin to consider all aspects of culture; we can consider how culture has developed for the survival and development of communities. We must begin to think about power. We must begin to think about context and place. And we must remember that cultural interactions and exchanges do not occur in a vacuum. They occur in relation to power, privilege, and history.

References

California Newsreel (prod.). 2003a. *RACE: The Power of an Illusion*. Video documentary.

———. 2003b. "Background Reading: Ten Things Everyone Should Know about Race." Online resource for *RACE: The Power of an Illusion*. Science tab. https://www.pbs.org/race/000_About/002_04-background-01.htm.

Coates, Ta Nehisi. June 23, 2014. "How Racism Invented Race in America—the Case for Reparations: A Narrative Bibliography." *The Atlantic*. https://www.theatlantic.com/politics/archive/2014/06/the-case-for-reparations-a-narrative-bibliography/372000/.

Cross, William. 1991. *Shades of Black: Diversity in African American Identity*. Philadelphia: Temple University Press.

Eberhardt, Jennifer. 2019. *Biased: Uncovering the Hidden Prejudice That Shapes What We See, Think, and Do*. New York: Penguin Books.

Helms, Janet E. 1990. *Black and White Racial Identity: Theory, Research, and Practice*. Westport, CT: Greenwood Press.

Johnson, Maisha Z. Sept. 1, 2017. "5 Things You Don't Realize When You Defend Cultural Appropriation." https://medium.com/@maishazj/5-things-you-dont-realize-when-you-defend-cultural-appropriation-98a700cc5d33.

Magee, Rhonda V. 2021. *The Inner Work of Racial Justice*. New York: TarcherPerigee.

Poston, W. S. Carlos. 1990. "The Biracial Identity Development Model: A Needed Addition." *Journal of Counseling & Development* 69, no. 2, 152-155. https://doi.org/10.1002/j.1556-6676.1990.tb01477.x.

Roediger, David R. 2010. *How Race Survived U.S. History: From Settlement and Slavery to the Obama Phenomenon*. London: Verso Books.

Tatum, Beverly. 2017. *Why Are All the Black Kids Sitting Together in the Cafeteria?* New York: Basic Books.

Sensing the Future:
Cultivating Transformation and Change Together

To our Dear BIPOC colleagues,

We would like to open our session today honoring folks of the global majority who have found their way to Waldorf early childhood education and have committed their lives to the great potentiality of this work.

We want to acknowledge that sometimes our very presence is an act and a deed. When we look down the hallways, very rarely do we see ourselves reflected. By day we don our aprons and seek to navigate the often choppy, murky, and deep waters of spaces predominantly occupied by white folks. We wrestle with what we need to find ourselves, define ourselves in the midst of a culture so deeply and unconsciously Eurocentric, that those who create, invigorate, and administer pedagogy do not recognize all who are left out in the quest to discover what is "universally human." We can find ourselves standing marginalized, on the outskirts, as well-meaning folks invite us to "fit in." But belonging seems so far away, and beyond our grasp. And yet we show up, with bright and shining faces, with joy in our hearts and abundant love for the children in our care.

We affirm each other, confide in each other, lift each other up.

We are working for the future. We are filling not only cow's horns, but conch shells, and gourds and drums, with our songs, with our stories, our humming, with our cadence, with our colors. We add ginger, peppers and yams, and tamari and cumin. And we plant it deep in the soil. Because we know it is not rich enough yet. It does not have enough minerals and nutrients to support the children who are coming. But we are planting, ever planting. Because we know they are coming and they are famished, ravenous to see themselves represented, affirmed, celebrated, and loved. And on our watch, they will eat well, they will grow strong, and they will be satisfied.

With boundless love,
Keelah

Meggan: I offer wise words from adrienne maree brown (2018)

radical gratitude spell

a spell to cast upon meeting a stranger, comrade or friend working for social and/or environmental justice and liberation:
you are a miracle walking
i greet you with wonder
in a world which seeks to own
your joy and your imagination
you have chosen to be free,
every day, as a practice.
i can never know
the struggles you went through to get here,
but i know you have swum upstream
and at times it has been lonely

i want you to know
i honor the choices you made in solitude
and i honor the work you have done to belong
i honor your commitment to that which is larger than yourself
and your journey
to love the particular container of life
that is you

you are enough
your work is enough
you are needed
your work is sacred
you are here
and i am grateful

Keelah: Stages of Development

Our active interest in one another, in the children, is a deed, an act of love. When love becomes an active verb it shows itself—it reveals itself—as interest. And that active interest, as dear Laurie Clark once told me—it has power, it has energy, it is alive and enlivening. And it is out of that love, that active interest, that we seek. We are called to sense beyond the veil, beyond what is right before us, to take in all that these little ones bring.

And when we lean in, when we engage, it is a lightening of a burden, it is a grace and a gift. It brings us closer to our goal; it brings us closer to our striving

How do we show up like this, how do we answer this call? The call from our children, the call from the world, and the call from the future—it is in how well we know ourselves. That is the wellspring. Who we are extends outwards, like rays of sunshine, into how we greet and care for and nourish and hold and love the children in our care.

But when our own growth and development is stunted, when there is a stagnation, an indigestion, a clogging up, part of us is unable to truly participate in that communion with the children.

Our vision becomes myopic; we are not truly seeing with all of our capacities. It is as if we are color-blind.

There is a narrowing, a "smalling," a retraction from what is, if we are not awake and aware and curious and interested and active in our gaze, in our openness to receive the gifts that our children offer.

And we cannot receive them, take them in, hold and nurture them, if we are not aware of this way of seeing and sensing.

Meggan: Antibias Education/Book Audit

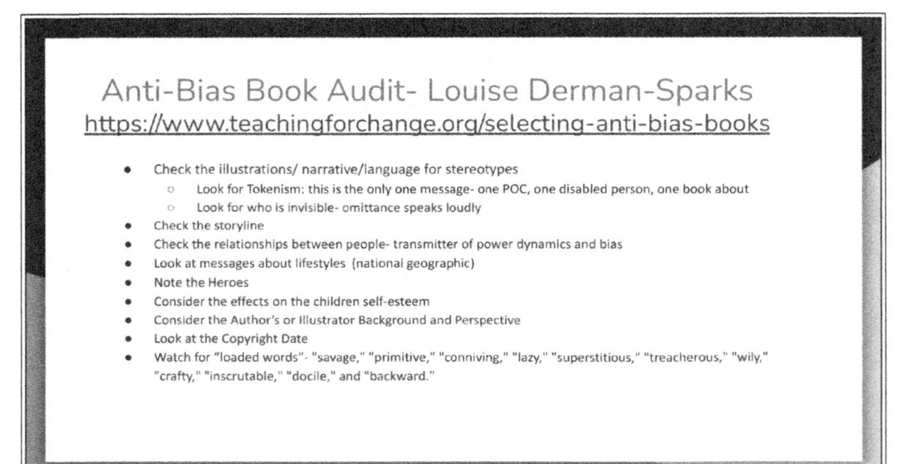

Identity turns the wheel of antibias education (ABE).

What does identity look like to you?

How would diversity look in your classroom?

What does justice look like to you?

What does action look like to you?

Keelah: Racial Identity Development in Children

Louise Derman-Sparks is nationally and internationally known for her work in early childhood education. Ms. Sparks is faculty emeritus of Pacific Oaks College and an author, teacher, and consultant on antibias education with children and adults. Ms. Sparks offers us a window to further understand children's experiences living and growing in a racialized society (Derman-Sparks 2012).

In considering the racial identity development of the children in your classroom or community, consider this perspective by an author whose name I have, unfortunately, not been able to find:

> *Take a look at your school's [or school movement's] founding and consider that it's likely that it was created for a specific population of students in mind. When you decided that the school you built for fish to excel would now open its doors to birds and bunnies, how did you change the environment so that birds and bunnies can excel? Did you adapt the environment to include air, space and meadows? Or did you simply expect that everyone would swim?*

Joaquin: Moving Toward Appreciation

Before moving to a conversation around cultural appreciation, let's return for a moment to the question of cultural appropriation. Cultural appropriation is the practice of taking elements of a community's cultural experience without proper knowledge and awareness, permission, and appropriate recognition or compensation. Although we often focus on the more obvious elements of appropriation such as monetizing, as in a famous fashion designer taking designs for elements of Indigenous culture and utilizing them in a fashion show, there are other aspects of appropriation that can be as problematic and painful. One form, nicknamed "cherry-picking," involves the taking of certain parts of a culture without understanding or sharing the entirety of a culture. Or, as often is the case with Black, Indigenous, and people of color, only certain stories or certain people are brought to the fore without sharing or exploring contemporary aspects of a community's experience. Another form is when dominant culture practices an aspect of the marginalized culture and is celebrated, while members of marginalized cultures who created the practice are punished; Black wearers of braids or "locs" (dreadlocks) are punished or degraded, for example, while white wearers are celebrated as unique or innovative.

It is important for us when exploring other cultures, particularly for the purpose of sharing them in the classroom, to attend to stereotypes, misconceptions, and errors in belief or the maintenance of racial hierarchies.

As mentioned before, my goal in these sessions has been to help us in developing our understanding of culture and moving toward practices of cultural appreciation. I have framed this thinking through the work of Dr Martin Luther King Jr. and his conceptions of power and love. The practice of cultural appropriation is often an exercise of power, a power without love that is reckless and abusive, a power that can oppress, suppress, and dominate. The move toward cultural appreciation is a love that is generative, that calls for relationship and community, and demonstrates a drive toward unification. This drive is not a force for conformity or assimilation, but rather a joy and celebration of the uniqueness of all peoples. To move in this direction, we must practice this love informed by power but also engage power informed by love. We must try to bring aspects of culture into our classrooms framed by the practitioners themselves—not structured through our own lenses of culture and reality but rather through the originators. We must remember that all aspects of a culture were created and adapted by groups of people to stay alive and to thrive in the world. And while some aspects, such as dances or regalia, may be displayed or shared now, these often originated as part of survival strategy or as a crucial component of a culture's existence.

There are some things we can do and some questions that we can ask when considering different cultures and their inclusion in our curriculum. Fundamental to this project is the need to be in relationship. If we are interested in Indigenous stories, we must engage the Indigenous communities that the stories originate from. Are we inviting or connecting to Indigenous communities for the purposes of classroom inclusion, while also seeking to be in reciprocity? Put another way, are we engaging communities in a balanced and equitable way, or are we only engaging communities when we want or need something from them? We must think about the elements of power involved when thinking about culture. Who is credited for the creation of the element;

has anyone been compensated appropriately? Are we contributing to the continued support and relationship of the community, or have we only taken something and given nothing back? Has the culture that we are seeking to share been freely given, or is it an element that we may have found and are using out of context? And am I attending to a key component of relationship, permission, and consent, or is my action one of entitlement?

We must think about context and place when engaging cultural inclusion. We have to ask ourselves whether we are "being local" to the communities and contexts around us and whether we are engaging the specifics of "my place in the community"? Or is our attempt at inclusion stretching beyond the appropriate context and potentially overlooking those in my community?

Finally, we must remember that cultural exchange does not occur in a vacuum. We often must contend with a history of racism and oppression when considering diverse communities. And we must know our history around the experiences of the communities around us. This includes the history of other schools or institutions taking from these communities, as well as acknowledging controversies or historic traumas of practices like mascots or other forms of cultural violence. When in a relationship with permission, we must also be ready to be told "no" and to accept that no for an answer. And while there may be conflicting points of view around inclusion of certain content or ideas, we must continue to explore and navigate.

The answer is not for us to disengage from communities completely. The going is challenging. The answer is also not to rely on safe or general history and culture at the expense of local context. Instead, we must consider how we enter into relationship with the communities around us and how we bring that rich diversity to the children who are in front of us.

And we'd like to close our work this weekend with a verse by Dr. Martin Luther King Jr. ([1968] 1994, 38) on power, love, and justice. Imagine we three speakers, we the authors of this keynote, Keelah, Joaquin, and Meggan, speaking these verses in turn.

Power without love is reckless and abusive and love without power is sentimental and anemic.

Power at its best is love implementing the demands of justice.

Justice at its best is power correcting everything that stands against love.

References

brown, adrienne maree. 2018. "radical gratitude spell." https://adriennemareebrown.net/2018/02/20/radical-gratitude-spell/comment-page-1/. Accessed September 12, 2022.

Derman-Sparks, Louise. 2012. "Stages in Children's Development of Racial / Cultural Identity and Attitudes." Notes for Sophia Lyon Fahs Lecture, UUA General Assembly. http://www.uuamherst.org/wp/wp-content/uploads/2017/01/Racial-identity_stages.pdf. Accessed September 12, 2022.

———. N.d. "Guide for Selecting Anti-Bias Children's Books." Social Justice Books. https://socialjusticebooks.org/guide-for-selecting-anti-bias-childrens-books/. Accessed September 14, 2022.

King, Martin Luther, Jr. (1968) 1994. *Where Do We Go from Here: Chaos or Community?* Boston: Beacon Press. https://www.uni-five.com/upload/doc/82818file.pdf.

Inner Work

Widening the Heart:

How Do I Make Love a Creative Force in the World?

Laurie Clark

We all have a longing to grow into our truest selves so that we can become revolutionaries of tenderness.

—*Gregory Boyle, founder, Homeboy Industries*

Polarization over political policies and many other aspects of the Covid-19 pandemic, along with the personal distress it has brought to so many, is challenging. Collective suffering due to racial, religious, and other forms of prejudice in our society is felt with great pain.

How can one person make a difference and a contribution to counter these challenges? Here is some good advice, often attributed to Mother Teresa: "Not all of us can do great things, but we can do small things with great love."

Every human being brings purposeful intentions with them into their life that are filled with resolve in order to serve humankind. Cultivating the inner life and striving toward personal "becoming" puts us on the path. How do we meet the difficulties and sufferings? How do we work with those? To ignore and plow through our struggles without consciously finding a way to work with them, is an expense to the heart. Richard Rohr, a Franciscan priest, reveals, "If we do not transform our pain, we will always transmit it" (Rohr 2016). Perhaps what will cultivate compassionate change in the world begins with our own transformation.

Gregory Boyle, the founder of the largest gang-intervention, rehabilitation, and recovery program in the world, gives this piece of advice about "active cherishing": "This therapeutic mysticism chooses love as the architecture of our hearts. The world will focus on outcomes or behavior. Love develops a warmth for everything that comes to it and rests in the center of it. To be nurtured is to be reverent for what is happening to you" (Boyle 2021). This advice from Boyle softens how we see things and leads to active cherishing.

The word "cherish" comes from the old French "cherir", meaning to hold dear, and from the Latin "carus," which suggests an active participation for one who is beloved. When we practice cherishing one another, an extending process occurs. To bathe a child in active cherishing is to hold them in loving enthusiasm, honoring their very existence. When the road to active cherishing is chosen, it opens the heart of the teacher and creates a warm, complete, and unreserved acceptance for the child. Widening the heart in this way means that no human being will be left out and everyone will have a seat at the table.

As teachers of young children, our task is to model what it truly means to be a human being. What we think and feel is transparent to little children, and they inwardly imitate us. Waldorf early childhood teachers bless the children in their care, treating them with dignity, recognizing the miracle of the spiritual being within each child. How very important it is to constantly develop our own spiritual nature to truly serve the children in our care. Teachers are asked to devote themselves to the children that come to us out of our knowledge and understanding. A radical striving to always keep cultivating and invigorating our inner life is essential. The children in our care depend on us to bring a match from spirit country and translate it into earthly language. Such work is challenging and calls for persistent determination and willingness to stretch and widen the heart.

I have found it so helpful to have a kind of spiritual map with clear touch-points for our development. Patrick Kennedy and Jonah Evans, the two directors of the Christian Community Seminary in Toronto, Canada, developed and gave us a sevenfold guide that opens an opportunity to deeply explore, step by step, a journey by which we allow ourselves to be shaped by seven spiritual imaginations of the spirit-filled self. I have attempted to bring their "Guiding Imaginations for the Priestly Self" as a map (Evans and Kennedy n.d.), and reworked it to create "Guiding Imaginations for the Teacher."

Interweaving these ideas, in my workshop presentation I brought biographical examples from Martin Luther King Jr.; the Bhuddist monk Thich Nhat Hanh; and Rabbi Abraham Joshua Heshel. The substance within these great individuals' biographies can flow into us as inspiration for our life and pour grace into our journey, bringing us moral and spiritual courage.

Martin Luther King and Thich Nhat Hanh had an astonishing friendship that is described in the book *Brothers in the Beloved Community* by Marc Andrus (2021). Both of these individuals, as well as Abraham Joshua Heshel, served as peace activists and delivered the message of acceptance for all people. Rudolf Steiner, the founder of Waldorf education, gives us the ground to stand upon through anthroposophy and true, spiritual guidance.

Thich Nhat Hanh made his life a landscape for evolving peace into the world. He wrote: "To have peace inside is a very basic need. Without it, you can't do anything to help others; but true peace in oneself is an everyday effort. We have to be able to recognize our suffering and learn how to transform it, to have the courage to go home to yourself" (Andrus 2021).

The seven guiding imaginations for the teacher that follow can bring us deeply into the story of our own lives, so that our truest self can emerge. Some pertinent questions to consider through this journey are: What am I really here to do? Do I make room for everybody? How can I best serve the children in my care? How can I bring peace to my heart and to others?

1. The Witness

Where am I right now? What happens each day? What went well? What do I need to work on, transform, heal, and cultivate? An exercise for teachers to strengthen this witnessing consciousness is to review the day backwards just before falling asleep. This gives us the opportunity to invite higher beings to be present and bring their insight into our sleep which can bring inspiration and understanding into our waking life.

2. Our Journey

Where have I come from? Where am I going and looking towards in the future? Look back and see how the experiences that have come to us in our life propel us forward. There is a part of me that knows that I needed these experiences, even though they were difficult ones. It is the butterfly's story; the dying caterpillar is born again into a winged creature of wonder. Dying to old ideas that don't work for us anymore, and making room for something new to be born within us, is also our story. In the words of Rudolf Steiner,"We must look forward with absolute equanimity to everything that may come. And we must think only that whatever comes is given to us by a world directive full of wisdom" (Steiner n.d.).

3. The Wounded Healer

What sufferings do we carry and how do we carry them? When we are able to build a relationship with life's sufferings and struggles, and look at them as a learning opportunity, we open ourselves to new possibilities. Each one of these opportunities can open us towards deepening and growing into our truest self. The sufferings we experience soften and expand us, help us to grow empathy for other people's suffering without judgement, and allows compassion to shine in. It is part of our education here on the earth that calls towards a deeper kind of love.

Martin Luther King calls for a "universal altruism"; altruism can be defined as a piercing insight that goes beyond tribe, race, class, or nation.

"Inner attitudes, general person to person relations and expressions of compassion are met by one's inner law, written on the heart. Man-made laws assure justice, but a higher law, produces love" (Andrus 2021).

4. The Helping Guide

We all need our spiritual helpers, we cannot do it alone. There is a guide in every soul, how do we become aware of the divine that can teach and shape us into a being of love? We all have a spiritual umbilical cord to our higher being. The spiritual world offers help when we ask for it. We can hear the voice of the beloved through prayer and a meditative life; these two are the medicine that we seek.

Martin Luther King puts it this way: "We are citizens of two worlds, the world of time and the world of eternity, we are paradoxically in the world and yet not of the world" (Andrus 2021).

5. Filling the Cup

As teachers of young children we can ask: Can we bring an inner atmosphere that sets our heart on fire with enthusiasm for life? The word "enthusiasm" comes from the Greek en (in) and theos (god), in other words, to be inspired by God in the depth of our being. The children in our care are looking for us to model what it means to be a human being carrying enthusiasm and gratitude for the gift of being alive here on the earth. Children imitate us, we are transparent to them. The children are thirsty to drink from the cup of life that we carry.

How do I fill this cup in the midst of my own personal sufferings? Where is the wellspring that we fill our cup with? Do we take the time to reach into the wellspring? When we reach into the well to fill our cup, is our spiritual practice giving us nourishment? Are we filling our cup with self-care? The point-periphery meditation given by Rudolf Steiner, in the book *Education for Special Needs* (2014), is valuable. It leads us towards finding the spirit in matter and the matter in spirit.

6. Becoming a Servant Leader

In the words of Martin Luther King, "Life's most persistent question is, What are you doing for others" (Andrus 2021). Can I be a guide and serve my brothers and sisters? Can I recognize the gifts that they are bringing? Can we witness ourselves and recognize our impulses in difficult situations with others? Are we able to travel into the other with true interest and hear their perceptions?

Thich Nhat Hahn advises us to help create a community of peace and true solidarity through learning to listen to others in a way that transforms anger and division, and to live in a way that makes a future possible. Taking this advice to heart, it is also important that we stand upright for the truth in uncomfortable situations and speak up. Take a noble stand for the truth. The late U.S. Congressman John Lewis puts this plainly: "When you see something wrong, do something, say something!"

Martin Luther King, a true service leader, said, "Any Christian [human being] who blindly accepts the opinions of the majority [, who] in fear and timidity follows a path of expediency and social approval[,] is a mental and spiritual slave" (Andrus 2021).

7. Love for the Deed

Jonah Evans and Patrick Kennedy ask us to consider the idea that "work for the sake of the deed and not for one's value in the deed is the goal" (Evans and Kennedy n.d.).

Are we weaving threads of love in what we choose to do? When we are tired at the end of a day of teaching, is it a "good kind of tired"? Can we put aside our impulses and desires for particular outcomes? The precious seed we plant when working out of selfless love for the children in our care is a profound deed. We become an allied companion to the children as they strive toward their own becoming.

References

Andrus, Marc. 2021. *Brothers in the Beloved Community.* New York: Parallax Press.

Boyle, Gregory. 2021. *The Whole Language: The Power of Extravagant Tenderness.* New York: Avid Reader Press.

Evans, Jonah and Patrick Kennedy. N.d. "Guiding Imaginations for the Priestly Self." N.p. Contact Jonah at the Seminary of the Christian Community. https://www.christiancommunityseminary.ca/.

Rohr, Richard. 2016. *A Spring Within Us: A Book of Daily Meditations.* Albuquerque, NM: Center for Action and Contemplation. Quoted material cited in "Transforming Pain" by the Center for Action and Contemplation, Oct. 17, 2018. https://cac.org/daily-meditations/transforming-pain-2018-10-17/.

Steiner, Rudolf. 2014. *Education for Special Needs: The Curative Education Course.* Forest Row, UK: Rudolf Steiner Press.

———. N.d. "We must look forward with absolute equanimity." Verse offered to anthroposophists circa World War II. See, e.g., "Did Rudolf Steiner Write the 'We Must Eradicate from the Soul' Verse?" by Daniel Hindes, March 17, 2020. https://danielhindes.com/blog/2020/03/17/did-rudolf-steiner-write-we-must-eradicate-from-the-soul/.

Additional Resources

Homeboy Industries. https://homeboyindustries.org.

Weihs, Thomas J. *Children in Need of Special Care.* London: Souvenir Press, 2001.

The "Spirit" in the Spiritual

Stephanie Hoelscher

Spirit moves in mysterious ways. As I woke from sleep on the eve of the 2022 WECAN conference, the path forward into the exploration of spirit we would take in our workshop emerged, so clear as to be self-evident.

For my workshop, "The 'Spirit' in the Spiritual," we first created the space for spirit. This must be done before we can talk about spirit. And we need to do that together; that is our first task. Creating the space for spirit asks us to see this moment as an invitation for collaboration that is a social, artistic, and spiritual act.

What does spirit need? Spirit needs light.

To kindle our inner lights as we take time to assemble our individual selves into a shared communion, I lit a candle for the workshop and read from *Calendar of the Soul* (Steiner 2022). The candle represents the spark of encounter—such as those everyday encounters between self and other, teacher and student, teacher and parent, colleague and colleague, stranger and stranger—the spark that makes possible surprise, delight, amazement, or wonder. These complex human emotions that take us outside and beyond ourselves are expressions of spirit. Spirit lives not in abstraction but in the blessedness of human encounters—when we are awake, open, and as curious as a young child.

This translation of *Calendar of the Soul* for week 45 comes from the Lili Kolisko Institute for Anthroposophic Medicine (2022). I include it with attention to how powerfully our times call for deep healing. This is our work as educators. This is our work as people. Attention to spirit is a therapeutic response to the deep challenges we all experience at this time.

Thought Power solidifies itself.
In alliance with the Spirit Birth
It brightens senses/vague excitements (stirrings)
Into full clarity.
If Soul-Fullness
Wants to unite itself with the World Becoming
Senses' revelation must
Receive the Light of Thinking.

Spirit needs a space, a particular space, a sacred space, where the "I" and the "we," the separate and the shared come together. How might we imagine this space? Two images have helped me to form a picture of how we might start to create a sanctuary of spirit. First, Nancy Blanning offered a hope for the future, a hope for the next one hundred years of Waldorf education and the building together of kinder and more compassionate society, describing the third space of the original Goethaneanum. Henry Barnes (2012) has written on this space. As I see it, this idea of a third space offers a place where the space between us becomes a place where the individual "I" and the collective "we," the separate and the shared, coexist. More significantly, it provides a space for respectful resonance where what connects is more powerful than what separates.

"Are you the carved shoreline and I the sweet water sea?" That is the wondering, seeking question of the indigenous poet Margaret Noodin (2020) that forms the second guiding image of a circle of belonging expansive enough to hold craggy rocks and silken seas in a shared embrace. Our circle of belonging includes, of course, children, colleagues, and families.

What does this third space for spirit need? How do we do this together?

Think of our work as Waldorf early childhood educators. This is what we do: we create a space for a supportive learning environment of belonging for all. Maintaining the space for spirit requires us to practice in each moment, in practical terms, the social, spiritual, and artistic work we do as Waldorf educators. Think of the life processes. Warming, breathing, nourishing, digesting. Think of the care and attention we give in our work to fostering a space of beauty, warmth, humor, and joy for our parent meetings. Our space needs a certain mood of the threshold, in a way. It needs a place for silence. Silence is spiritual. It is a form of speech that ennobles conversations by giving thought a space to unfurl. There is a wonderful illustration by the children's book illustrator Maurice Sendak that shows a child sitting alongside a small stream with the caption, "Everyone should be quiet near a little stream and listen" (Sendak 2001). Our space needs us to be attentive to our inner state of being and what is coming in from others. It needs a spaciousness of time as well.

So where do we start? We start with the "I." We bring ourselves as a separate "I" first. We then flow from the separate to shared, from "I" to "we" through voice and breath, and then we expand outward out of the space and into the world in our imaginations and through our senses.

This roadmap for grounding, settling, warming—that is what's needed to create space for spirit.

Spirit needs inner calm that can come from a meditative practice or ritual that helps us move away from things that distract us so that we can settle down into the simplicity of mystery. Spirit needs silence. To inspire us to move together into that quiet place during the workshop I chose "The Prayer" by Faisal Mohyuddin (2018), which brings us the image of turning toward and into the buttery light of a lamp for grounding. Our nervous systems beg for images like this right now.

Let's take a pause from all the things that distract and distress us, that deplete us, in order to tend to our inner gardens, which are in need of replenishment. With this poem I encourage you to settle down into the warmth of the words to find mystery. What helps you hold yourself together? What lamp offers you its warm, buttery light? Whatever that might be, turn toward that.

Prayer

Faisal Mohyuddin

you cleanse   the uncovered
regions   the of your body
then stand   at the foot
of prayer   mats facing

the qibla   unfasten
your cluttered   mind
from the tangible   hold of secular
trances   bow down

before   the cascading
glow of God's mercy   submit
to a centripetal   course toward the gates
of a more perfect   emptiness

here   now
you can plunge   into the most secluded
chamber of the soul   commune
with your share   of the universe's

initial burst of   light eternal light
housed within the lamp   of mystery
waiting   to be
beheld   five times a day

References

Barnes, Henry. 2012. *The Third Space*. Chatham, NY: AWSNA Publications.

Mohyuddin, Faisal. 2018. "Prayer." In *The Displaced Children of Displaced Children*. London: Eyewear Publishing.

Noodin, Margaret. 2020. "Gimaazinibii'amoon (A Message to You)." In *What the Chickadee Knows*. Detroit, MI: Wayne State University Press.

Sendak, Maurice, illustrator. 2001. *Open House for Butterflies* by Ruth Krauss. New York: HarperCollins.

Steiner, Rudolf. 2022. *The Calendar of the Soul 2022–2023*. Translated, arranged, and with commentary by Ross Rentea, MD, Mark Kamsler, MD, and Andrea Rentea, MD. Hartland, WI: the Kolisko Institute.

Additional Resources

Dickinson, Emily. "'Hope' Is the Thing with Feathers." In *The Poems of Emily Dickinson*, edited by R. W. Franklin. Boston: Harvard University Press, 1991.

Wright, James. "A Blessing." In *Above the River: Complete Poems and Selected Prose*. New York: Farrar, Straus and Giroux, 1990.

Deepening Our Reflective Practice to Develop Culturally Sustaining Pedagogy

Amber Chavez

As Waldorf educators, we know the value in reflecting on our work with the children. A reflective teaching practice is at the core of what we do. Developing an anti-bias, anti-racist teaching practice requires deep identity work grounded in an understanding of how systems of oppression were created, are sustained, and operate within society. As an educator, I have found that reflective practice helps me to think critically about my decisions and interactions within the classroom. There are multiple understandings of reflective practice (Zeichner 1994, 9–27). I use the term to describe the process of combining an examination of formative schooling and personal life experiences, an understanding of pedagogical theory, and an awareness of the cultural and socio-political context to critically reflect upon my personal classroom practice. By combining these three elements, I am able to examine my classroom practice in ways that are deeper and more meaningful than looking at any of these elements individually.

Early in my journey to become an early childhood educator, I was introduced to the concept of *praxis*. I struggled to understand this concept, but returning to the term again and again, my relationship to the word shifted. I began to understand praxis as one of the most profoundly meaningful concepts not just in my work as a teacher, but in my life as a conscious human being. Sometimes simplified to be synonymous with practice, praxis can best be understood as the reflective teaching practice which emerges from the reciprocal nature of action and reflection (Freire [1970] 2018). The reciprocal nature of action and reflection leads us through this process: we take an action, reflect on it, and then act again. The word reciprocal comes from the Latin words for back (re) and forward (pro). It refers to a relationship between two things which act as both cause and effect. In praxis, action and reflection are like two dance partners who take turns leading and following. In praxis, action and reflection learn from one another, moving us towards a more liberatory practice.

I presented a workshop that introduced the core principles of culturally sustaining pedagogy. We practiced using self-reflection and community discussion as tools for the inner work required to develop an anti-racist, anti-bias teaching practice. Like the workshop, this article is not meant to be purely theoretical nor purely practical. Rather, it is intended to serve as a tool to guide your praxis—your thinking and your action. Reflective exercises are included throughout to support you on this journey.

I invite you to read this article as a self-led workshop. Gather a pen, colored pencils, and writing and drawing paper. Pause while reading this article to notice and reflect on what it brings up for you. Take notes as you encounter new ideas or helpful reminders. Consider questions such as these throughout:

- Where do you agree or disagree with the concepts?
- Which parts do you want to bring into your teaching practice?
- Have you seen examples of these concepts in practice in your school or classroom?
- Can you remember something from your own childhood schooling experiences that relates to what you are reading?

I have added intentional places throughout this article where you can pause and reflect. I've included questions to prompt your thinking. I encourage you to respond to these ideas and questions with journaling or artistic expression. You might set a timer and free write (anywhere from 2 to 8 minutes). Then pause, read what you wrote, and spend another minute or two writing or reflecting on that process before moving on to the next session. Or give yourself some time to draw a response to one of the questions. When you are finished, jot down a phrase or a few sentences to capture your thoughts.

Remember this dance of action and reflection—bring your ideas into action in your life or your classroom. Afterwards, reflect on how it went. What did you feel went well? What might you do differently if you could do it over? If you could do it again? What did you learn from the experience? How do you think this action was experienced by others around you (children or adults)? What impact might it have had on them?

Culturally Responsive Pedagogy

Understanding culturally responsive pedagogy requires understanding the critical theories from which it emerged. Critical theories are those which name inequity and demand action. Critical theories must be "explanatory, practical, and normative" (Bohman [2005] 2021, par. 3). To be explanatory, critical theories must analyze societies in ways that identify what is wrong and how to change it. To be practical and normative, these changes must be realistic and values-based. Within the field of legal studies, critical theories were used to examine the ways that laws create and perpetuate inequities within society. Legal scholars created frameworks such as Critical Legal Studies and Critical Race Theory to analyze and explain how laws and social issues interact with one another. Critical theorists within education built on these ideas to understand how educational systems and institutions do the same.

Critical Theories and Color Muteness

Critical legal studies (CLS) built on critical theories to argue that law and politics could not be separated because the ways laws were written and implemented created hierarchies and domination while hiding power dynamics (Chayes et al. n.d.). A key component of CLS is that of indeterminacy—that the making and application of laws are not a clear and simple matter of right and wrong but rather complex decisions which attempt to balance competing interests and influences (Unger 1983).

Critical race theory (CRT) built on the idea of indeterminacy to critique the idea of neutrality and color blindness within the law and "how such claims are enacted to maintain White supremacy and power" (Farmer-Hinton et al. 2013). Critical race theory explicitly names the ways that race interacts with the law and posits that color-blind ideology is not the absence of racism but rather a new form of racial ideology (Bonilla-Silva 2015).

There is a growing understanding among teachers of the pitfalls of color-blind ideology within teaching. Phrases like, "I don't see color" deny the cultural richness—and the social challenges—that exist for students of color and their families. The idea that "I can teach anyone" without an acknowledgment of the need for culturally specific knowledge leaves teachers without the skills and capacities to truly meet the needs of students of color. Growing up Latina, I felt seen by my teachers only when they acknowledged my cultural heritage. Race is not a biological reality, but it has profound social implications. Color-blind ideology is also harmful because when we can't see race, we also can't accurately perceive the way that racism operates.

This explains how color blindness is "a new form of racial ideology." When we pretend that race is not a factor—not because we have truly eliminated supremacist ideologies, but because it is no longer polite to speak of them in the same loud and open ways—we hide the causes of racial disparities within our society from ourselves. Color blindness is a refusal to name the systems, structures, and histories that created these disparities and continue to sustain them. The result is a belief system that must instead place the blame within communities, cultures, or on individuals.

Similar to the "not seeing" of color blindness, color muteness refers to an inability to speak about race and racism (Pollock 2009). When we are uncomfortable speaking about race, we often talk around it or use coded language. Being unable to speak about race leaves us unable to speak about racism. It leaves us unable to name and discuss the effects of racism. This is the new racial ideology named by Bonilla-Silva. If race cannot be seen or named, then the effects of systemic and institutional racism are wrongly attributed to individual choices or cultural deficiencies.

Critical race theory is a body of work that describes the relationship between race, racism, and the law. It gives us language to name and understand how racism operates within the legal system. It provides a way of understanding that race is socially constructed and legally reinforced through a system which seeks to hide power relationships. It is a framework for understanding how the legal system uses language that appears to be race neutral but in fact creates and reinforces white supremacy and white privilege. Three of the central tenets of CRT hold that: (1) Race is socially constructed and socially significant, (2) Racism is endemic to our society, and (3) Racism is embedded in our institutions and codified in our laws (George 2021).

Pause and Reflect

- How does this history and explanation of Critical Race Theory compare to what you have heard in the news?
- How has color-blind or color-mute ideology shown up in your teaching practice or school? What kinds of coded language have you used or heard used to avoid speaking openly about race?
- How comfortable are you speaking about race? When do you find it easy? When do you find it difficult?
- Can you think of a time when someone didn't notice your racial, ethnic, or cultural heritage? What was that experience like for you? How might your position in society affect this?
- When has someone seeing or naming your racial, ethnic, or cultural heritage been painful? When has it been beneficial?

Culturally Relevant, Responsive & Sustaining Pedagogies

Culturally Relevant Pedagogy (CRP) was developed by Gloria Ladson-Billings as a framework to connect micro and macro understandings of the intersections between culture and teaching in an effort to "define and recognize" effective teaching practices for African-American students (1995). Culturally Sustaining Pedagogies (CSP) builds on her work with African American children to "incorporate the multiplicities of identities and cultures" that exist both globally and within American schools (Paris and Alim 2014, 82).

Ladson-Billings conducted an extensive ethnographic study of eight exemplary teachers—those considered excellent by both community members (African American mothers) and professional colleagues, including their principals. From this study, she identified three core principles of effective teaching: academic achievement, cultural competence, and critical consciousness. Cultural competence refers to the ways that we support the ability of students to retain and sustain their own culture while learning about others. Critical consciousness refers to our ability to analyze social issues, name power structures, generate solutions, and take action to solve problems.

Each of the elements— academic achievement, cultural competence, and critical consciousness—are skills that children will build throughout their lives. Yet important foundational work for each of these skills occur within early childhood. Consider a parallel to teaching literacy that demonstrates how academic achievement is supported in the Waldorf early childhood classroom. Although Waldorf education waits until 1st grade to formally introduce reading, kindergarten teachers carefully incorporate elements to support reading and writing through songs, stories, artistic work, and movement. These activities, in addition to supporting the young child in their current development, support phonemic awareness, sequencing, fine motor development, and sensory integration.

Acknowledging the foundational work of Ladson-Billings, Paris (2012) points out the lack of meaningful action since her original publications. Paris suggests the term Culturally Sustaining Pedagogy is part of "equally explicit resistances that embrace cultural pluralism and cultural equality" (93). Relevant is replaced with sustaining to be clear and direct about the need to value and maintain a democratic "multiethnic and multilingual society" (93). Ladson-Billings (2014) responded positively to this new conceptualization, describing how her ideas were "misread and misunderstood" (82) and describing how, in practice, culturally relevant pedagogy has been repeatedly stripped of its core elements and reduced to superficial cultural representation within the curriculum. Although multi-cultural representation within the curriculum is an important part of any classroom, it does not in itself constitute culturally relevant teaching.

This helps to distinguish between pedagogies which are culturally responsive and those that are culturally relevant and culturally sustaining. Culturally responsive pedagogies are an essential element of any classroom. Responsive pedagogies speak to schooling students in culturally appropriate ways and can include elements such as representation in images and dolls, building on students' knowledge and experiences, and incorporating elements of culture such as food, stories, and festivals into the classroom. When Ladson-Billings talks about her work being "misread and misunderstood," she is talking about reducing culturally relevant pedagogy to these culturally responsive elements without including the three core principles she identified in her work.

Pause and Reflect

- Consider the difference between multi-cultural/culturally responsive teaching and pedagogies which are culturally relevant and sustaining. Are any of these methods of teaching areas of strength or potential growth for you?
- What does the importance of academic achievement in culturally relevant teaching mean for a Waldorf early childhood classroom? How might we begin to resolve the tension held in this statement?

- How can we incorporate the multiplicities of identities and cultures in ways that are respectful and culturally competent? How might you build your own cultural competence in order to increase your capacity to bring multicultural education to your classroom?
- How can you increase your own critical consciousness to be able to recognize social inequities? How might you begin to set the stage for young children to learn the foundational skills for solving real-world problems?
- How does your own identity and the identity of the children and families you work with influence your willingness or ability to engage in this work?

"Fair Is Not the Same"—Cultivating Equity in Education

In the kindergarten classroom, we attend to the balance of individual and group needs, providing each child with the care that is appropriate to their needs while caring for the needs of the class as a whole. Two children may come up to the teacher with small injuries that need emotional care rather than medical attention. In this case, I might work with the two children to attend to each child's specific need. If one has a scratch, we can notice this together and provide a Band-Aid. Another child has a bump and receives a small "boo-boo buddy" ice pack. Children naturally understand receiving different care in this situation.

At other times, a child may see someone in class receiving something that they are not. They protest with, "That's not fair." An in-depth explanation of why another child might need something that they don't is often not necessary or appropriate. Instead, I respond with a simple, "Fair is not the same," and we move on with our work or play. These situations begin to illustrate the concept of equity in education. Education equity is an emerging goal that builds on our previous understanding of the need for equality.

When we give each student the same resources, or an equal distribution of those resources, this is called equality. When we instead give each student what they need, we are working towards equity. According to the Due East Educational Equity Collaborative, "Educational equity emphasizes the needs, experiences, and outcomes for underrepresented or marginalized students" (2022, par. 7). Because of the historical legacy of racism and ongoing actions and attitudes within society, equity requires that we directly address exclusion and inequity. Culturally Relevant Pedagogies provide a roadmap for attending to the educational needs of children of color. Culturally Sustaining Pedagogies, with their explicit attention to cultural pluralism and cultural equality, speak to the needs of all students to learn about and value their own culture as well the cultures of others.

Transforming Action: Maintaining the Critical Edge

> *When a word is deprived of its dimension of action, reflection automatically suffers as well; and the word is changed into idle chatter, into verbalism, into an alienated and alienating "blah." It becomes an empty word, one which cannot denounce the world, for denunciation is impossible without a commitment to transform, and there is no transformation without action.*
>
> (Freire [1970] 2018, 87)

Recall that a distinguishing feature of critical theories is the call to action and transformation. When working from a critical lens, it is not enough to notice inequity or understand how unequal outcomes are created and sustained. Critical educators use their understanding to identify changes and take action. When we speak about inequity without taking transforming actions in response to our knowledge, we speak what Paulo Freire calls, "empty words" and "idle chatter." When we learn about social challenges without working towards solutions, our praxis is interrupted. If we take no action, then we have nothing to reflect on, and we can't move forward in our equity work.

Instead, we seek to create change through our praxis. The purpose of the final part of this workshop is to identify the actions you can take to create change. Before identifying the steps you want to take, consider your sphere of influence and control. There may be many issues in the world that you want to change. On a smaller scale, there may be challenges within your school, classroom, or home program that you want to address. Begin to think about which of these issues are within your direct control. Consider also those which you have some indirect control or influence over. Positionality affects the level of control and influence we have in various situations. This might be social positioning such as your race and gender. Or it might be the position you hold as an educator—someone who is a department chair will have a different level of influence and control than an assistant just beginning training.

Pause and Reflect

- Does the call to transformative action resonate with you? Have you encountered this concept in other teachings you find wisdom in?
- What areas of your teaching practice do you have influence over?
- Which do you have direct control over?
- If you have positional power, consider the impact of this power on equity. Do you have the authority to make decisions that will meaningfully increase equity in your school? Can you find ways to share power with those around you who hold marginalized identities?
- Brainstorm a list of areas you would like to see change in. Identify potential areas and actions within your sphere of influence or control.
- Identify three changes that you want to move forward with. For each of these three, consider:
- What resources would you need to make the change happen?
- Who else might be involved?
- What support or resistance do you anticipate?
- What is a reasonable timeline for enacting these changes?

Willing or Wilting

As we come to the end of the workshop, I want to tell you how proud I am of you! This can be challenging work to engage with. Notice how you're feeling—invigorated, exhausted, irritated, rejuvenated? In this workshop, you learned about critical theories, equity, and culturally relevant pedagogies. You explored ideas of color muteness and praxis and transformative action. To end, we will make a concrete plan that includes action and reflection. But first, I would like you to consider the idea of willing or wilting (Gorski & Dubose 2022). Imagine yourself as a plant in need of water. Allow your shoulders to slump as the plant begins to droop and wilt. Now, imagine the plant is watered and begins to perk up. Straighten your posture, feel the sun on your skin, and feel yourself strong and ready to grow. Take a deep breath and release the feeling of the plant. Now, consider engaging with equity work. Do you feel willing or wilting? What care might you need to support your growth as you move out of this workshop into real world action?

Praxis: Action and Reflection

- Review your list of potential changes.
- Choose one short-term and one long-term action to take.
- Record the required resources, your planned timeline, and anticipated outcome.
- Based on the planned timeline, identify when you will reflect on the actions you chose.
- Consider the concept of willing or wilting. How will you support your willingness to grow and act for equity? This might be an inspirational passage you reread, a colleague you check in with, or some other individual or community support you can put into place.
- Throughout the practice of enacting the change, journal your reflections.
- Did the change have the expected implementation and outcome? What surprised you about the process?
- If you could do it over, what might you change or keep the same? Will you continue the process as planned or update your implementation? Why?

References

Bohman, J. (2005) 2021. "Critical Theory." In *The Stanford Encyclopedia of Philosophy*, edited by Edward N. Zalta. Spring edition. Stanford: Stanford University Press.

Chayes, A., et al. n.d. "Critical Legal Studies Movement." *The Bridge*. https://cyber.harvard.edu/bridge/CriticalTheory/critical2.htm. Accessed August 18, 2022.

Due East. 2022. "Educational Equity Defined." Due East Educational Equity Collaborative. https://dueeast.org/educational-equity-defined/. Accessed August 18, 2022.

Farmer-Hinton, R. L., J. D. Lewis, L. D. Patton, and I. D. Rivers. 2013. "Dear Mr. Kozol . . . Four African American Women Scholars and the Re-Authoring of Savage Inequalities." *Teachers College Record: The Voice of Scholarship in Education* 115, no. 5: 1–38.

Freire, P., M. B. Ramos, I. Shor, and D. P. Macedo. (1970) 2018. *Pedagogy of the Oppressed*. 50th anniversary edition. New York: Bloomsbury Academic.

George, J. 2021. "A Lesson on Critical Race Theory." *American Bar Association Human Rights Magazine* 46, no. 2.

Gorski, P., and M. DuBose. January 2022. Equitable Educational Leaders Institute, Session 1–4 [online training]. Equity Literacy Institute.

Ladson-Billings, G. J. 1995. "But That's Just Good Teaching! The Case for Culturally Relevant Pedagogy." *Theory into Practice* 34, no. 3 159–165.

———. 2014. "Culturally Relevant Pedagogy 2.0: aka the Remix." *Harvard Educational Review* 84, no. 1: 74–84.

Paris, D. 2012. "Culturally Sustaining Pedagogy: A Needed Change in Stance, Terminology, and Practice." *Educational Researcher* 41, no. 3: 93–97.

Paris, D., & H. S. Alim. 2014. "What Are We Seeking to Sustain through Culturally Sustaining Pedagogy? A Loving Critique Forward." *Harvard Educational Review* 84, no. 1: 85–100.

Pollock, M. 2009. *Colormute: Race Talk Dilemmas in an American School*. Princeton, NJ: Princeton University Press.

Unger, R. M. 1983. "The Critical Legal Studies Movement." *Harvard Law Review*, 561–675.

Zeichner, K. M. 1994. "Research on Teacher Thinking and Different Views of Reflective Practice in Teaching and Teacher Education." In *Teachers' Minds and Actions: Research on Teachers' Thinking and Practice*, edited by Ingrid Calgren et al. London: Falmer Press.

Decolonizing our Pedagogy through Critical Self-Reflection

Aimee de Ney

The time is ripe to collectively create a new, anti-racist culture that centers the earth and supports us in remembering our rightful place in the ecosystem of life. As early childhood educators—and Waldorf educators—we are on the front lines of imagining this new world. What do the children in our care need to know, experience, and be held by as they move into a transformational future? How do our ways of being, relating, and knowing need to shift so that we are prepared to usher them into the uncertainty that lies ahead, socially and ecologically? In this chapter, I will discuss steps we can take to embark on this journey together, recapitulating the workshop I presented at the 2022 WECAN conference entitled "Decolonizing Our Pedagogy through Critical Self-Reflection."

I appreciate having the opportunity to share the research I am doing for my doctoral studies at Antioch University on decolonization and transformation of our systems and structures, external and internal, through education. Years ago, I began to turn to the land as my primary teacher. This term "land" is, in my mind and experience, multifaceted. It includes the ground we stand upon and all of the beings that inhabit the land, including but not limited to the air, water, soil, microbiome, plants, animals, and humans. It includes the energies and spirits of the land and of these beings, the ancestors, relationships, stories, and the future unfolding. In short, it means Mother Earth and all the beings who are a part of her.

Learning to listen and relate with the land and its inhabitants, the suffering being experienced by all motivated me to enter the doctoral program with the intention of developing a pedagogy that centers the earth as a response to the climate collapse we are experiencing and perpetuating through our collective lifestyle and worldview. One year into my studies, my perceptions and understanding of how we got to where we are now has blown wide open and has me questioning many of the assumptions I have lived with as a white U.S. citizen and as a Waldorf teacher. This time is calling for us to choose either to accept the inequities of our culture, or to work toward radical transformation for a loving and healing future for all, including but not limited to humans.

I am a white, cisgender, straight, able-bodied settler woman of Irish, Polish, and German descent teaching predominantly white children. We live in the land of the people of the Treaty of Medicine Creek of 1854–peoples that were displaced and integrated onto the Squaxin Island, Nisqually, and Puyallup reservations of northwest Washington State. As a settler on these lands that are suffering as a result of our colonizing lifestyle and worldview, I am committed to doing all I can to generate love and healing for the land. This starts with my own inner work of critical self-reflection and coming to understand how settler colonialism and its systems have shaped me, my worldview, and my ways of being, and committing to healing and transforming myself and supporting and inspiring those within my sphere of influence to do the same.

To properly discuss decolonization, particularly in the context of the conference workshop, I would ideally be working with Indigenous colleagues. It is my hope that continuing down the road of anti-racism, decolonization, and racial identity development, this ideal will become a reality. Until then, I will continue to do the work. As Resmaa Menakem states in his important and healing book *My Grandmother's Hands* (2017), white people need to develop a white anti-racist culture. A first step in collectively creating new ways of being and relating together is to learn the truths of our histories and relationships with land, each other, and our self, and relate these truths to our own beliefs, assumptions, and actions. Doing so takes courage and a commitment to grounding, centering, and purposefully working toward embodiment in order to metabolize our discomfort and unsettling. This is the work needed for the transformation we are being called to.

Unsettling Settler Colonialism

North American countries are the products of settler colonialism. Colonialism is the invasion of a land and people by outside forces for the extraction of goods, resources, and wealth–including humans. Settler colonialism does the same except the invaders stay, claim the land as their own, attempt to eradicate Indigenous peoples, their ways of being, languages, and worldview, replacing them with those of the colonizers. Central to settler colonialism is the fact that the land was stolen from Indigenous peoples and claimed as property rather than kin. Settler colonialism is a structure that is both insidious and invisible. It is the fabric of our society. It dictates our relationship to land and to each other. It is alive, active, and thriving.

Woven within the fabric of North American settler colonialism is the triad settler-native-slave. This is particularly dominant within the United States. This triad is visible to this day as dominant white supremacist ideology, Indigenous erasure, and anti-Black racism. While this triad doesn't quite express the complexity of peoples and experiences living today, it is the foundation upon which our systems were built.

Our country was founded in order to secure wealth and power for white men, by stealing land and claiming it for personal ownership, and stealing Black bodies to work the land and build white wealth. This is currently seen in plain sight in recent rulings by the U.S. Supreme Court, in anti–CRT (critical race theory) laws, and in restrictive voting measures designed to disempower and subjugate communities of color.

Inherent in the settler-native-slave triad is the removal of peoples from lands. While the stories of humans are complex and this supposition is overly simple, there is truth in it. European settlers left ancestral homes in order to take lands in which they could create a new life and amass wealth. African peoples were stolen, separated from their ancestral lands, and forced to work stolen land to fill the coffers of their white oppressors. And, again, Indigenous peoples were stripped of their ancestral lands and violently forced into submission and poverty or assimilation into settler culture. Thus land is enmeshed with racialized trauma.

White-supremacist ideology is the law of the land. This means that white is the standard against which all else is judged. Laws, policies, and systems have been put in place to ensure white (male) domination of wealth, land, power, and status. Systems of hierarchy, separation, classification, competition, and meritocracy are some of the myths of the American dream that keep us bound up in white supremacist ideology. Whiteness gave itself the power to dominate Black and Indigenous bodies, and likewise gave itself the power to dominate and own land, treating land as resources and wealth to be extracted instead of as an ecosystem of which we are but a part.

To assure the appropriation of lands, Indigenous peoples needed to be erased. This was first attempted through genocide and then through forced assimilation into dominant white culture. Some examples of this attempted erasure, after genocide, are the internment of peoples onto reservations, often far from their homelands; destruction of and removal from food sources; eradication of languages and culture; the stealing of children first to boarding or residential schools and now to the foster system. At this moment, there is a movement to dismantle the 1978 Indian Child Welfare Act (ICWA), which requires that native children be given preferential placement in their family or tribe when removed from their homes. By not being in relationship with local Indigenous peoples or acknowledging their present, modern existence, but confining living peoples to a romanticized version of the past, we are further committing this erasure and violence.

Our society was built by stolen Black-bodied people and was structured to perpetuate oppression and undue hatred and fear of Black bodies.

The wealth of the United States was built on chattel slavery, and laws and systems are maintained to this very day to enforce inequity and violence. Learning the stories of this land through the lens of settler colonialism is critical for all Americans, because we have been raised in mythologies that were created to justify chattel slavery, Indigenous erasure, and white dominance. Without learning the truth, we cannot think critically and transform our ways of being, knowing, relating, and educating our future generations toward a future of liberation of lands and peoples.

Cartesian Dualism and the White Supremacist (Western) Worldview

Looking back at the history of white European domination of lands and peoples and how we have come to this day, in which we forget that we are all interrelated, the work of philosopher René Descartes stands out as an articulation of white dominance through a long history of separation of humans from the natural world. Descartes's thinking was instrumental in propagating the separation of the mind from the body, nature from culture, and other binaries that dominate Western thinking and relating. His system of hierarchy dominates Western thought to this day, leading to the present-day pandemics of the killing of Black and Brown boys and men, murdered and missing Indigenous women, the disparate rights of men and women, and the destruction of lands and waters leading to climate collapse, among others. Descartes taught that mind and body are separate–the mind being superior to the flesh; culture superior to nature; the separation of the races with whiteness being superior to other races; colorism; sexism; homophobia; ableism; and the list goes on.

The work of Descartes justifies and solidifies white supremacist ideology and the dominance of whiteness and maleness. It can be seen as a relatively modern root of the binary systems of gender, race, sexuality, and good and evil; it teaches us that to be part of the earth is unsavory and unsafe. This leads to feelings of isolation, making collective action seemingly impossible, perpetuating white dominance, and likewise the ongoing destruction of lands and Black and Brown bodies. In inspecting and uncovering Cartesian dualism, we find the enmeshment of racial and earth justice, and the understanding that by finding our collective right relationship within the land, we humans can find our unity in dismantling the systems of oppression that keep us separate from each other.

Decolonization and Moves to Settler Innocence

In the workshop, we spent considerable time looking at decolonization– the repatriation of Indigenous lands to Indigenous peoples– and what scholars Eve Tuck and J. Wayne Yang call "moves to settler innocence" in their seminal work "Decolonization Is Not a Metaphor" (2012). Simply stated, these moves toward innocence are:

I. Nativism—Imagining oneself native to a place, when, in fact, most of us are not. "Settler nativism is about imagining an Indian past and a settler future" (Tuck and Yang 2012, 13).

II. Settler adoption fantasies—"Settler fantasies of adoption alleviate the anxiety of settler un-belonging. He adopts the love of land and therefore thinks he belongs to the land. He is a first environmentalist and sentimentalist, nostalgic for vanishing Native ways. In today's jargon, he could be thought of as an eco-activist, naturalist, and Indian sympathizer" (Tuck and Yang 2012, 15).

III. Colonial equivocation—"Equivocation is the vague equating of colonialisms that erases the sweeping scope of land as the basis of wealth, power, law in settler nation-states" (Tuck and Yang 2012, 19).

IV. Free your mind and the rest will follow—While cultivation of critical consciousness is crucial, "until stolen land is relinquished, critical consciousness does not translate into action that disrupts settler colonialism" (Tuck and Yang 2012, 19).

V. A(s)t(e)risk people—"This comprises a settler move to innocence because it erases and then conceals the erasure of Indigenous peoples within the settler colonial nation-state and moves Indigenous nations as 'populations' to the margins of public discourse" (Tuck and Yang 2012, 22).

VI. Re-occupation and urban homesteading—"The beliefs that land can be owned by people, and that occupation is a right, reflect a profoundly settling, anthropocentric, colonial view of the world" (Tuck and Yang 2012, 23). "Urban homesteading . . . is the practice of re-settling urban land in the fashion of self-styled pioneers in a mythical frontier. Not surprisingly, urban homesteading can also become a form of playing Indian, invoking Indigeneity as 'tradition' and claiming Indian-like spirituality while evading Indigenous sovereignty and the modern presence of actual urban Native peoples" (Tuck and Yang 2012, 28).

In order to begin to heal, understanding that our racialized trauma is wrapped up in the trauma of the land is an important place to start. Checking out our own relationship to land, colonization, and moves to settler innocence is deeply unsettling and important work to begin a healing journey. The land is willing to teach us if we are willing to learn how to listen (with more than our ears) and enter into practices of critical self-reflection for the good of all.

Critical Self-Reflection

As a movement, are we willing to look critically at anthroposophy and Waldorf pedagogy? Are we willing to root out the white supremacist ideology and issues of colonization, particularly as we more regularly move outside and into "nature-based" contexts? It takes courage and collective willingness to be vulnerable and question everything that we hold dear. But if equity and justice are our goals–the liberation of lands and peoples (human and otherwise)–we don't have a choice. Otherwise we will perpetuate the systems that are harming us all.

In the Decolonizing our Pedagogy workshop, participants split into breakout rooms to discuss how a few topics match up when compared to settler colonial white supremacist, patriarchal, capitalist ideology and culture. The groups were named: holding the child at the center; fourfold-ness; archetypes and elementals; and forest kindergarten and festival life. As one can imagine, with the time allotted to these big topics, we barely scratched the surface. Since then, I have been considering these topics and thoughts as I transform my own teaching and ways of being and relating. I will address each topic here in brief, with hopes of inspiring further discussion.

Centering the child—In Waldorf schools we hold the value of centering the child in our work, from curriculum development through administrative decisions. Otto Scharmer, an anthroposophist, MIT professor, co-founder of the Presencing Institute, and author of *Theory U* (2016) and other books on this topic, wrote an article in which he created a rubric of different operating systems (OS) and how they function in various sectors of society (education, agriculture, economics, healthcare, and so on). In education, OS 1.0 was equated with the authoritarian approach to education; 2.0 to the standards-based approach; 3.0 to learner-based; and 4.0 to ecosystem-based (Scharmer 2016). Centering humans, though preferable to centering standards, promotes an anthropocentric approach to education, and anthropocentrism is a trait of white supremacist ideology. By centering the land and decentering the human, we can teach our youth that they are not the most important, and we can together strive to learn what centering the land and finding our rightful place in the ecosystem of life looks like. Does this mean we do not need to see and meet the needs of each child? No. In fact, I believe that the land insists that we do, but with cultural humility and within the context of the whole.

Fourfold-ness—Last winter solstice I was deep into becoming unsettled, learning about decolonization and examining my place within settler colonialism—on top of having two papers due for my doctoral program while teaching and running a small school. I was working with developing liberatory, earth-based curriculum and had avoided singing the song "The Four Lights of Winter" without thinking too deeply about this choice. Then, all of a sudden, there I was at the end of a beautiful and connected Winter Spiral of Light festival. I realized I had not planned for this moment and we needed to end by harmonizing with each other, best done in that moment by singing a song together. And so I sang "The Four Lights of Winter" as I have for more years than I care to count. My eyes were shining, I was smiling, looking at the families around the spiral, feeling like a hypocrite because this song separating rocks from plants from "beasts" from humans, placing one upon the other, is hierarchical. The categorization of life initiated by Aristotle and developed by Linnaeus two thousand years later has separated us from our interrelatedness and perpetuated the illusion that we are separate and not part of the ecosystem. And so I continue to critically reconsider fourfold-ness in the context of settler colonial white supremacist culture and worldview.

Archetypes and elementals—Are we perpetuating archetypes that are consistent with the land upon which the children are growing? Or are they based in white supremacist, patriarchal ideology? For example, think of the witch. Do we present the witch archetype as a wise healer connected to the land, or as an old woman who inspires fear and eats children? What does this teach our children about their elders? About women? About those in reciprocal relationship with the land? How about the king archetype? Are we not teaching the glorification of hierarchy and of capitalism? Is there someone present on the land that can teach benevolence and wisdom? Situated here on the shores of the Salish Sea, I think of the Mountain, Tahoma, and of Banana Slug, traditionally revered as a wise leader.

Likewise, who are the elementals we are presenting, and do they really live within the land upon which the children are growing? Are elementals universal, or are they connected to the land? Do the salt water and the fresh water have the same spirit, or the Pacific and Atlantic oceans? Who is living here, as opposed to in Europe or, more specifically, Scandinavia? By learning reciprocity in listening and relating with the land, these questions can find answers.

Festivals and outdoor education—There is a lot happening within our movement regarding festival life. I presented ideas on this at the 2021 WECAN conference, and multiple workshops and articles were presented in 2022 as well. Can we learn to listen to the land, and perceive the relationship between the cosmos and the land? Steiner did good work making this accessible. I will ask the difficult question here, however. Are we willing to look critically at Christianity and its role in settler colonialism? What can we learn from the land on which we live with regard to the cycles of life and the seasons through observation, perceiving, and relating?

As we continue to transform our pedagogies and practices toward outdoor, forest education, it seems time to critically inspect our relationship to colonization and to land. How can we end the cycle of violence of colonization? Are we perpetuating the history of settler entitlement to land, or are we acting in service of the land and her peoples to bring forth a healing and loving future? Are we willing to look toward unsettling ourselves and the (settler) children in our care toward developing honest, loving, responsible, and reciprocal relationships with the land and her peoples? As we find with teaching anti-racism, our young children are connected and ready to be joyful participants in transforming culture.

Embodiment Practices

Looking at our educational and philosophical practices through the lens of settler colonialism is a lot to process, to sit with, and to be unsettled by. Learning to regulate our nervous systems, and to ground, center, and embody all of the feelings is where healing can begin to take place. Resmaa Menakem writes about clean pain and dirty pain. Attending to this work will generate clean pain, and from this place we can grow collectively and imagine new futures. Avoiding this hard work is the expectation of settler colonialism, and our relatives—BIPOC folk, lands, waters, species—are bearing the brunt of it. But in reality, we are all suffering collectively and it is up to us to find new ways of being that uphold each other and refuse to partake in the ways of settler colonialism and its white supremacist ideology. While the term "silence is violence" has become commonplace, it is truth. When we engage in critical self-reflection, learn the stories of the land and of our relationship and responsibility within our collective story, and work to heal our internalized racialized trauma in service to the land and the (supposed) other, we begin the work of healing that is needed for the survival of all.

In Closing

Waldorf education was founded on the premise of transforming society. One hundred years in, we continue its founding mission. So many aspects of Waldorf pedagogy and practices are supportive of developing a new, anti-racist culture: consensus decision-making; a tradition of inner work, meditation practices and self-reflection; embodiment and sensory development practices; integration of the physical, emotional, and spiritual; a culture of storytelling; and our explicit love of Mother Earth and interest in the unknown and unseen. These are a springboard from which to continue our practices of personal, pedagogical, and cultural transformation.

After the 2022 WECAN conference, I was in touch with a couple of colleagues with whom this work particularly resonated. We talked about forming a working group looking at what it means to center the earth. I invite anyone who would like to enter into this conversation to be in touch with me at birdsongoly@gmail.com. Let us do the work of creating anti-racist, earth centered culture together!

References

Menakem, R. 2017. *My Grandmother's Hands: Racialized Trauma and the Pathway to Mending Our Hearts and Bodies*. Illustrated edition. Las Vegas: Central Recovery Press.

Scharmer, O. 2016. *Theory U: Leading from the Future as It Emerges*. San Francisco: Berrett-Koehler Publishers.

———. 2019. "Vertical Literacy: Reimagining the 21st-Century University." Field of the Future blog post. https://medium.com/presencing-institute-blog/vertical-literacy-12-principles-for-reinventing-the-21st-century-university-39c2948192ee.

Tuck, Eve, and K. Wayne Yang. 2012. "Decolonization Is Not a Metaphor." *Decolonization: Indigeneity, Education & Society* 1, no. 1: 1–40.

The Two Way Mirror:
The Me Looking at Itself and the Me Looking Out into the World

Rihana Rutledge

The inspiration for my workshop, "The Two-Way Mirror," at the 2022 WECAN conference was Maurits Cornelis Escher's self-portrait, *Hand with Reflecting Sphere* (1935). Escher created this image in Rome, shortly before returning to his homeland in the Netherlands. The image depicts both the mirror and its reflection. The mirror represents the realistic, detailed drawing of a hand holding up a glass sphere looking in at a figure and his belongings in the background; the reflection, a figure looking out from the glass sphere with his belongings in the background; the figure is in the glass sphere being mirrored and reflected at the same time. This dual perspective of mirrored and reflected is like a two-way mirror.

The signature of our time calls on us to deepen our understanding of self and of our interactions with others. To make us agents for conscious change toward a kinder, more compassionate society; to inspire healthy interpersonal relationships, life will hold up mirrors reflecting how we act and react. Examining these mirrors we may discover something about ourselves from two viewpoints: the "me looking at self" and the "me looking out into the world."

The workshop explored how the people we meet in life can be our mirror; it is through the other that we are able to self-reflect, grow, and change our beliefs about ourselves and about others. A two-way mirror has transparent glass on one side (we can see through it); on the other side is a mirror in which we see our reflection. Mirrors, like our encounters with others, can allow us to be transparent and at the same time self-reflective. In ancient times, mirrors were considered sacred and mystical objects. Today we are confronted with an overabundance of glass and mirrors in our environments. We see our reflection more times in a day than we realize. Mirrors are magical catching our attention; we could become self-absorbed with our own reflection asking, "Mirror, mirror, on the wall, who's the fairest of them all." Mirrors can also deceive: Think of the dog carrying a stolen piece of meat crossing a footbridge; seeing his reflection in the water below, reflective like a mirror, he thinks he sees another dog with a bigger piece of meat. He jumps into the water, snapping at his reflection, lets go of the meat in his mouth and loses it in the stream. Mirrors can make us pay attention to some of our recurring habits, to view what is mirrored to us or what we are mirroring to others. "Imitation is our most fundamental social skill. It assures that we automatically pick up and reflect the behavior of our parents, teachers and peers" (Van der Kolk 2015, 114).

According to Aristotle, the human being is the most imitative of creatures. Before the change of teeth, the child imitates all that occurs in their physical environment. The child's physical organs are shaped by the sense impressions they receive from the environment. In the first seven years of life, the child is more influenced by adults' actions and reactions than by admonition or instruction. Rudolf Steiner describes the child as a "perfect mimic," predisposed to health or disease later in life depending on the quality of their imitative life in early years. It is essential for the child that adults in their environment be worthy of imitation because the child is sensitive to the impressions and gestures mirrored in their environment. According to Steiner, for the child to become a good imitator, parents, teachers, and peers must work on their inner development, practicing good judgement and social emotional well-being. For the child to become a good imitator, parents, teachers, and peers must work on their inner development, practicing good judgment and social emotional well-being.

In *The Body Keeps the Score*, Bessel Van der Kolk (2015) explains that "the frontal lobes are also the seat of empathy—or ability to 'feel into' someone else." And "specialized cells in the cortex" known as mirror neurons, explain our responses to "empathy, imitation, synchrony and even the development of language" (58). They attune us to other's emotional states and intentions and make us vulnerable "because trauma almost invariably involves not being seen, not being mirrored, and not being taken into account. Treatment needs to reactivate the capacity to safely mirror, and be mirrored by others, but also to resist being hijacked by other's negative emotions" (59).

Understanding how these mirror neurons, specialized cells in our brain, allow us to learn through imitation by responding to body language, facial expressions, and emotions of others, plays an essential role in a child's social life, development, and education. It is critical as caring adults that we reflect on our inner life and self-development. How we mirror to young children our gestures and emotions can affect their health, social and emotional well-being right through to adulthood. It is essential to be worthy of imitation for the children. Before we can foster clarity of thought, empathetic feeling, and compassion in children, we must first nurture these qualities in ourselves.

The First Artistic Invitation: Reflection

Following a warm welcome and introductions, the workshop activity was to go back in time and look into our early childhood mirror, reflecting on the place where we were born and raised, the people who surrounded us, and the environment we landed in, then writing a brief paragraph starting with the words "I am from . . . ."

As a small group we listened attentively to each other sharing these diverse reflections. They were very profound and each story was personal and sacred, and full of cultural richness. A common thread in some of our shared reflections was the quality of play experienced as young children: play was uninterrupted and unsupervised by adults. There was a sense of timelessness and freedom, sparking joy, wonder, and other emotions."Child-initiated play lays a foundation for learning and academic success. Through play, children learn to interact with others, develop language skills, recognize and solve problems, and discover their human potential. In short, play helps children make sense of and find their place in the world" (Alliance for Childhood n.d.).

For some, this kind of introspection can open a Pandora's box of unpleasant childhood memories. Taking courage to share develops empathy, and not wanting to share requires respect. The mental pictures we make of the sense impressions received from the physical environments we lived in and the people we grew up with sometimes can bring up pleasant or unpleasant feelings. Unresolved thoughts and feelings may surface when reflecting on the people we imitated or mirrored in our early years. Examining how some of these reflections impact our social behaviours, interactions, and relationships can help us understand what needs to be revealed, understood, healed, or transformed.

The Second Artistic Invitation: Mirror

This was an activity intended to strengthen our observation skills. A journey to the past, visit a place where we grew up, recall a memory of any physical mirrors there. Remember the smallest of details, such as shape, color, and size. Where was it? What memories does it bring back? This activity creates objectivity in our observation, learning to separate our thoughts from our feelings and emotions. In reflecting and recalling an object from our past with vivid imagination, we acquire skills needed to become objective. To be objective, we must become the observer, observing without being influenced by our emotions or thoughts. Practicing consciousness, paying attention to details, we develop a sense of calm and the ability to be quiet and listen to the other.

In *Walking between Worlds: The Science of Compassion* (1997), Gregg Braden proposes, "Ancient calendars indicate that we are living the completion of a grand cycle of human experience. Within the last years of this cycle, we have been asked to accommodate greater change in less time than at any other point in recorded human history. Our bodies, immune systems and emotions have been challenged to unprecedented levels. At the same time, science is witnessing [a] phenomenon for which there are no reference points of comparison. Two thousand year old texts remind us that compassion is an accessible state of awareness determining the quality of our well being." Braden goes on to describes the Essenes as a community of mystics and holy people who lived between 150 BCE to 70 AD along the Dead Sea. They outlined in their ancient texts, seven mirrors of relationships, called the Seven Essene Mirrors and how these mirrors can be used for self- reflection in our daily lives, of our interactions with others and with the world around us. They can help make sense of our experiences, behaviors, choices and actions.

The Seven Essene Mirrors of Relationship

1. The first mirror is of human relationships in the present moment. This mirror represents what is reflected in me by others.

2. The second mirror of human relationships tells us about the biases and judgments we hold toward ourselves and others.

3. With the third mirror of human relationship we recognize and understand our attraction to people who embody the things we have lost, things we are seeking to make us feel whole or complete again.

4. This mirror of relationship allows us to see ourselves in the presence of addiction or compulsion. When we recognize our compulsive and addictive behaviors we discover that we have given away, little by little, the things we hold most dear.

5. This mirror of relationship reflects back to us why we lived the kind of life we lived and relates to our parents' influence in our lives, the actions our parents mirrored to us, our beliefs and expectations of the relationship between ourselves and our Higher Self.

6. This mirror of relationship provides the opportunity to find balance and mastery after losing everything, we see ourselves in a new light finding courage and strength to climb out of the abyss.

7. This mirror of relationship invites us to allow for the possibility that, regardless of its outcome, each life experience allows us to see perfection within our imperfections.

The Third Artistic Invitation: Seven Mirrors

For each one of the seven Essene mirrors of relationship we chose a different color, shape, or drawing to represent each of the mirrors using colored pencils, pastels, or paint. With imagination, we looked at the seven colored images in the picture we created and looked at what is emerging. Taking inspiration from the first artistic invitation, our written reflection "I am from . . . " we brought its essence into the picture using color or drawing. Looking at the picture again we noticed what was forming, and then spent some time integrating the colors and drawings to complete the picture. For the final step, intuition, we began by looking at the picture, then connecting to it, with closed eyes allowing its image to slowly vanish from our thoughts, bringing awareness into the heart space, opened our eyes, looking at the picture, recalled the first words that came to mind. In closing, each person was invited to share their pictures and words.

Reflective Practice

To help us be more conscious in our encounters, Rudolf Steiner suggested practices and exercises for awakening interest, acquiring objectivity, and increasing our self-understanding of people and events in our lives. Practicing the "review of the day" exercise, or "Rückschau," where we review each day's events backwards in the evening before going to sleep, then take thoughts emerging from the review into sleep. Upon awakening in the morning, we reflect on new thoughts, ideas, or awareness arising from the night's sleep.

In *Dance of the Spirit* (1991), Maria Harris writes, "In our imaginations, it helps to look forward to our day, or backward upon it in the evening, and try to remember all the people we have met and places we have been—and then to ask ourselves in what way our standing with them has been a standing on holy ground. It helps even more if, whenever we go into a room, or walk into a store, or say hello to another . . . or have a meal with a friend, we remind ourselves that the meeting, at this place the sacred can be found" (17).

Finding the sacred in the spaces between our social encounters to be inclusive and acknowledge our differences requires wisdom and understanding of who we are, where we have come from, and where are going. We all do not respond to the world around us the same way, we often bring different views to the table. How we weave our destinies together in the social fabric of life to find the sacred demands an openness to meet the other with genuine interest and authenticity. Awakening to who we are, we can take a look in the mirror and reflect on our shared responsibilities for a kinder, more compassionate society. Seeing beyond self, we see the other.

References

Alliance for Childhood. N.d. "Time for Play, Every Day: It's Fun—and Fundamental." Fact sheet. https://static1.squarespace.com/static/5d24bb215f3e850001630a72/t/5d3773c653eb780001d65099/1563915206277/Time+For+Play+Everyday.pdf. Accessed September 6, 2022.

Braden, Gregg. 1997. *Walking Between the Worlds: The Science of Compassion.* Bellevue, WA: RADIO Bookstore Press.

Harris, Maria. 1991. *Dance of the Spirit: The Seven Steps of Women's Spirituality.* New York, NY: Bantam Books.

Steiner, Rudolf. *The Education of the Child: And Early Lectures on Education.* Great Barrington, MA: Anthroposophic Press.

Van der Kolk, Bessel. 2015. *The Body Keeps the Score: Brain, Mind, and Body in the Healing of Trauma.* New York: Penguin Books.

Additional Resources

Aristotle. *The Poetics.* See, e.g., http://www.authorama.com/the-poetics-1.html. Accessed September 6, 2022. Text on the imitative nature of the human is in chapter 4.

Escher, Maurits Cornelius. *Hand with Reflecting Sphere.* Lithograph, 1935. See, e.g., https://en.wikipedia.org/wiki/File:Hand_with_Reflecting_Sphere.jpg. Accessed September 6, 2022.

The Art of Conversation

Holly Koteen-Soulé

There is a certain irony in exploring the art of conversation in this format (this workshop was held on Zoom). We have had to stretch ourselves, however, during this period during which our in-person interactions have been curtailed. We brought all that we learned in the past to this session in hopes of transcending the limits of the medium.

The Context for Our Workshop

The topic of the social arts and of conversation as an art has been of interest to me for many years, especially since media technology has become a bigger and bigger part of our lives. I wanted to know how this was affecting young children, even if they are not yet using social media themselves. This interest led me to studying attention—that very basic aspect of our human consciousness of which we are often unaware, in particular, how it has been co-opted in our digital society and how the diminished quality of attention is affecting the health and development of our children. This research led naturally to the question of what is happening to our capacity to engage with one another in a more than superficial way.

Symptoms of our social difficulties are in the news every day. They have been exacerbated by long periods of isolation and the accompanying anxiety and fear in relation to the pandemic. Despite these ongoing challenges, the pandemic also brought out genuine acts of kindness from individuals. In time we may here will discover other gifts and learnings from this challenging period as well.

What is relevant to our exploration today is the question of what can happen in a face-to-face encounter. Do you remember the deep joy at your first face-to-face reunion with family or friends after the initial lockdown?

The quality of face-to-face conversation is multi-dimensional, in contrast to the flat experience of meeting on Zoom. (I am sure that you are all aware of the importance of multi-dimensionality for the learning and development of the young child.) We were sometimes able to bring a deeper dimension to our online meetings by recalling past encounters or by cultivating a particular quality of listening, of listening with more than our ears. Digital media has been eating away at our capacity for conversation for quite a long time, long enough for a few researchers to start sounding alarm bells.

I found an important ally in a researcher from MIT, named Sherry Turkle. She was the author of *Alone Together* in 2017, and in 2016 wrote the book, *Reclaiming Conversation: The Power of Talk in a Digital Age*, about the dangers of turning to our phones instead of one another. She says in *Reclaiming Conversation* (2016): "Face-to-face conversation is the most human and humanizing thing we do."

With regard to children, her warning is clear: "Time in simulation gets children ready for more time in simulation. Time with people teaches children to be in relationship, beginning with the ability to have a conversation."

What is being lost? Turkle proposes, "What is lost is practice in the empathetic arts. . . . Conversation is on the path toward the experience of intimacy, community, communion . . . toward reclaiming our most fundamental human values" (2016). These include:

- The capacity to be vulnerable, present, and open to another person
- The capacity to listen and feel empathy with another human being
- The capacity to learn from and collaborate with others
- The capacity to be alone, hear, reflect, and know ourselves better

"We struggle to pay attention to one another and what also suffers is our ability to know ourselves" (Turkle 2016).

Relationships that are built on superficial connections and edited online communications do not have sufficient depth and resilience to support us in working through real crises, growth, change, and transformation. That is why I feel that this topic is central not only to Waldorf education, but also to this period of our reawakening to cultural and social justice issues and to reexamining what we do in the light of these issues.

We cannot know, see ourselves, make conscious changes without talking with others whose experiences are different than ours. We need to be in dialogue, in conversation in order to:

- Recognize our differences and our commonalities;
- Learn from one another about our unconscious biases;
- Cultivate empathy and compassion;
- Learn how to work together to create solutions and new ways of being

As early childhood educators, we need, above all else, to be worthy models for the children in the building, tending, and healing of human relationships.

In a lecture in 2017, Michaela Gloeckler spoke about the social-emotional foundations of the first three years that accompany the physical milestones for the young child. In the first year, the child wants to be seen; in the second year, to be heard; in the third year, to be recognized.

For me, these three human needs—the wish to be seen, to be heard, and to be recognized—underlie every human interaction. Every heartfelt conversation can be a kind of recapitulation of and a potential healing for those early experiences. This is the wonder and revelation of true conversation, including conversation with oneself.

Exercise 1

In pairs, for about ten minutes, we shared about a time in which we felt seen and heard so deeply that we discovered something about ourselves, when something hidden was allowed to come forward in the conversation. These could be conversations that happened when we were children, or young adults, or recently. We shared only what we were comfortable with sharing. A few participants then shared briefly with the whole group. We focused on how attention is an expression of love.

Exercise 2

For ten minutes, we drew or depicted a true listening space. We shared with the group about the qualities of the space we created.

Marjorie Spock writes, "The Art of Goethean Conversation is a little booklet that was very significant in my work as a colleague and faculty member" (1983). She quotes from Goethe's Fairy Tale: What is more glorious than gold? Light. What is more quickening than light? Conversation. She likens attentive listening to crossing the threshold into the world of living thought. Deep listening allows thoughts that the speaker has never articulated before to arise within the warm light of the listener.

Rudolf Steiner defined conversation as the archetypal human phenomenon. It was his experience that when one is listening, one falls asleep to oneself, and when one is speaking, one wakes up to oneself; there is a kind of natural breathing between speaker and listener. To work consciously with this allows us to more readily experience life from another's perspective while we are listening and for others to give us the kind of listening that allows us to share our own perspective from a deeper, more open, and less reactive place.

Exercise 3

In groups of two or three, we shared an experience in which we felt "other," left out, or that we did not belong. Again, this was from a childhood experience or a more recent experience. We then shared our experiences with the group.

How do we create the listening mood in ourselves and in our work with the children, families, colleagues, and in the school community?

Questions can be a doorway, especially if they are truly open-ended, come out of true interest, and are not statements in disguise!

Thinking/attention: Can we let go of multi-tasking and our personal agendas?

Feeling: Can we listen with open heart; can we listen without prejudgments?

Willing: Can we allow our empathetic responses to lead to new thoughts, feelings or actions?

Exercise 4

We formed groups of four, assigning a scribe for each group, and asked ourselves: How can we apply what we have experienced in this workshop and in this conference to building more inclusive communities in our schools?

Our responses included the following:

- Welcoming new families
- Parent evening activities
- Building collegiality and trust in the EC or full faculty
- Helping children learn to speak honestly and kindly to one another
- Modeling conversation at specific times during the daily rhythm
- Working with families to strengthen mealtime and mealtime conversation opportunities at home

Healing conversation is sometimes wordless, a gesture, being with, feeling with, accompaniment. A therapeutic story can live very deeply in the children because they can live into the images and gestures as well as the words.

Discovery of "Expressive Resonance" in the newborn is a picture of our inborn social nature. Discovery of mirror neurons in the brain reflects our capacity to be with and empathetic with our fellow humans. According to Rudolf Steiner, when I speak your larynx moves and vice versa.

Every conversation represents the possibility of an encounter: we meet one another; we meet more of ourselves; we meet a deeper sense of our true humanity.

In **healing**, I am in conversation with my bodily elementals.

In **gardening**, I am in conversation with the elemental beings and the forces of nature (in my house or classroom, also).

In **review** before sleeping, I am in conversation with my spiritual helpers.

In a healthy **faculty meeting**, we are in conversation with the "Being" of the school.

References

Gloeckler, Michaela. 2017. Lecture on the first three years. Author's notes.

Spock, Marjorie. 1983. *The Art of Goethean Conversation*. Waukesha, WI: St. George Publications.

Turkle, Sherry. 2016. *Reclaiming Conversation: The Power of Talk in a Digital Age*. New York: Penguin Publishing Group.

Additional Resources

Turkle. 2017. *Alone Together: Why We Expect More from Technology and Less from Each Other*. New York: Basic Books.

Understanding Our Children

Meeting the Child at the Midnight Hour:

Self-Knowledge as the Roots for Working with Diverse Communities and Young Children

Chiaki Uchiyama

When we work with young children's hereditary streams, queer streams, or both, it is helpful for teachers and caregivers to strengthen their inner connection with themselves and their own spiritual origin, so that when they meet with children within the context of contemporary culture, they can embrace the children's hereditary (karmic) and spiritual streams simultaneously at the heart level. In this workshop, we tried to expand our imagination into a spiritual midnight hour, our point of spiritual origin, and embrace and value the unique manifestations of earthly identity as important assets for human evolution. We touched base with the mission of biracial, bicultural, and bilingual children from the standpoint of the midnight hour as well. This consciousness can help bring healing impulses and unconditional, etheric warmth in everyday education.

I began my presentation by showing the two pastel drawings below. Figure 1 depicts the condition of the human being on earth; in Figure 2 is shown the human being at the midnight hour. On earth, the world consists of "I" and "not I" (other), and we fully understand neither "I" nor "not I" (other). "I" is disconnected from the world, thereby allowing for the possibility of humanity attaining freedom. During earthly life, we are confined in the space within the skin, awake in the material world of semblance (Maya), dreaming in the planetary world, and sleeping in the realm of the fixed stars of the Zodiac. "Who am I?" is a deep mystery—know thyself, and thus know the world. At the midnight hour, by contrast, according to Rudolf Steiner's lecture "The Ego Consciousness of the So-Called Dead" (1916) we are the cosmos except for the space within our skin. We are everything but this tiny void on the earth.

Figure 1. The Human Being on Earth

Figure 2. The Human Being at the Midnight Hour

The Mission of Human Beings on Earth

During our two-hour workshop, we explored diversity, equity, inclusion, and justice (DEIJ) from this midnight-hour point of view. At the midnight hour, we are one with everything. That is our spiritual origin. However, in order to incarnate on earth, we were assigned to a specific body, hereditary stream, sex, culture, and language to serve the world in a unique way and thereby fulfill our individual destiny and mission on earth. Therefore, when we are born, and our body separates from the yolk sac, chorion, allantois, amnion, and fetal part of the placenta, we become divorced from everything except our assigned body. Figure 3 shows an assigned body (human figure) placed on the fetus. In Figure 4 are shown the assigned body on the fetus and the "unassigned" parts of the universe placed on the other membranes—yolk sac, chorion, allantois, amnion, and fetal part of the placenta. That which is lost at the time of birth remains as an etheric echo around us. Our ultimate mission on earth is to encounter and learn from diverse "others," from whom we were divorced when we were born, to evolve our individual consciousness and attain universal consciousness. The more we incorporate the "self "(fetus) with the "other" (placenta), the more we become whole and free. In the workshop, we each reflected on the particular significance of our assigned body and heredity stream and their meaning on this journey, as well as our experience of meeting with our "placenta."

Figure 3. The Fetus Adopts Its Assigned Body

Figure 4. The Fetus in Relation to the Parts from Which It Will Separate

We proceeded with questions on four different ways of meeting each other as a part of an inclusion study. Our main focus was to recognize "self" through the first stage, then consciously evolve into the fourth one, the sacred marriage, which is the birth of transdisciplinary consciousness and the new, mutual, higher "I."

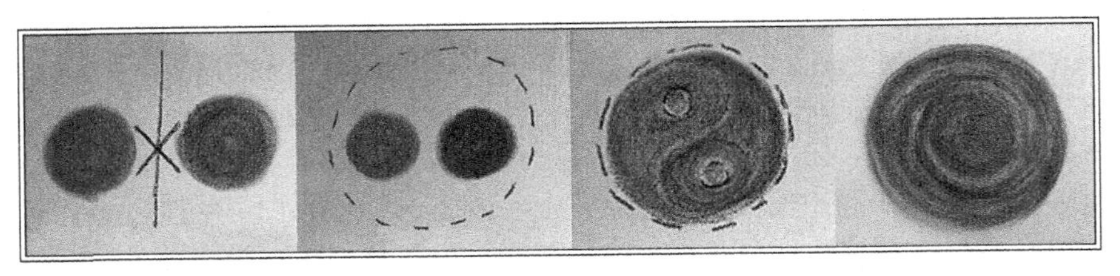

Figure 5. I "vs" Other; I "and" Other; I "with" Other; the Sacred Marriage, or the New "I"

Power Dynamics and Equity

Our work together uncovered an array of institutional power dynamics within Waldorf schools. There are not only white vs. BIPOC and cisgender vs. transgender dynamics, but also "lead teachers vs. assistants," "class teachers vs. subject teachers," "experienced teachers vs. new teachers," and "teachers vs. parents," to name a few. Do we recognize these unspoken cultural power dichotomies in everyday life? How are we bringing equity to those who are marginalized and feel oppressed? How are we dealing with intersectionalities—an assistant of color or a transgender new teacher, parents who are both marginalized in society and challenged financially, an administrative leader of color, a white assistant teacher, and so on?

There are so many complexities we need to consciously tend to. During our time together we explored our sense of being superiors and inferiors to see the world through two different lenses. Through this process, we soon realized that while we might tend to experience the world through our sense of inferiority, other people see our superiority or power.

We also focused on pain and did some physical exercise to facilitate a paradigm shift that empowered us to acknowledge our pain.

Questions Raised by People in Marginalized Groups

1. There are many layers of habit which demonstrate elitism in Waldorf schools, wherein people feel as though they are treated as "second class citizens." Is the school aware of this?
2. Is my voice valued? Am I seen and understood? Or am I expected to simply assimilate into Waldorf culture and lose my personal identity?
3. There are unspoken taboos thoughout the system. Am I alone in seeing this? Am I allowed to voice them?
4. How can they be voiced without risking my job or destroying relationships?

Figure 6.

Figure 7. Part A

Pain and Suffering

Pain and suffering make us awake.
Pain and suffering make us compassionate.
Pain and suffering train our muscle of resilience.
Pain and suffering inspire us to change the world.
Pain and suffering keep us evolving.

From the Cosmic "I" perspective, pain and suffering are gifts and opportunities, not deficits, if we have not succumbed to the dangerous temptation of being a victim.

Value of Marginalized Voices

Awaken us to shadows and biases
Awaken our compassion
Inspire resilience
Inspire change
Represent voices from our collective "placenta"

From the Cosmic "I" perspective, marginalized voices are gifts and opportunities, not deficits, if we do not succumb to the temptation to treat others as victims.

Figure 7. Part B

Development of "Identity"

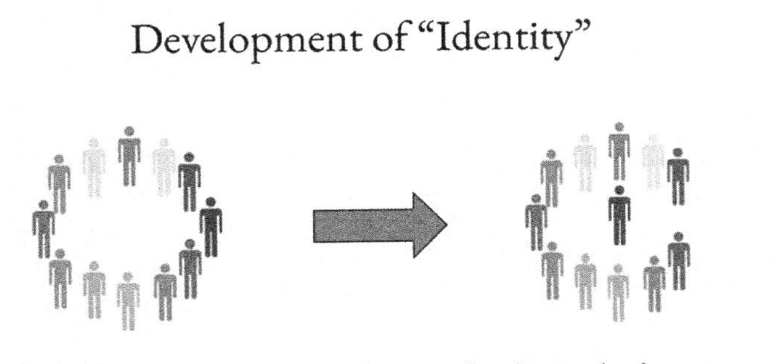

Each child has their own tempo and process for identity development.
Different cultures have different orientations towards identity education.
Identify where the child (and the family) is at.
Identify what is outer and what is inner.

Figure 8.

Birth to Seven

Genius (cosmic wisdom) in the head.
Learning the outer world through imitation.

Bottom-up (how to think) education slowly wakens what is already sleeping in the head.

Keep the genius intact as much as possible.

Support development of the limbs and strong organs.

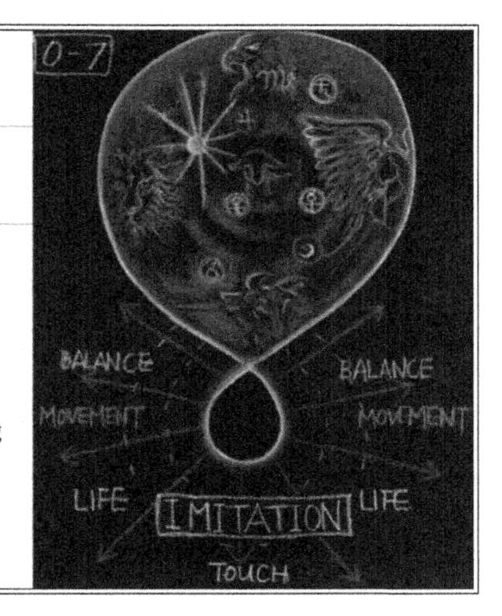

Figure 9.

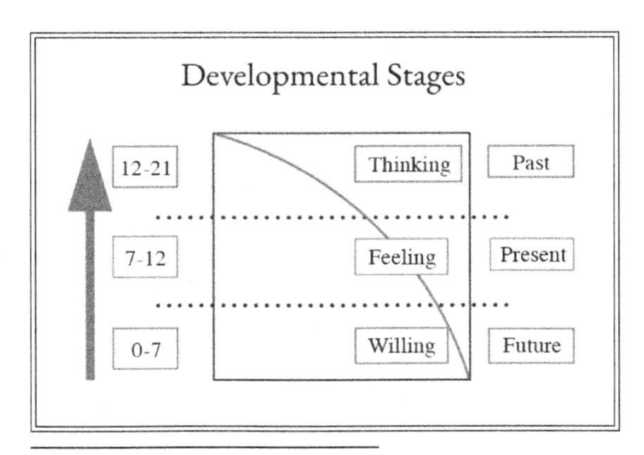

Figure 10. From 0–7, education for Willing; children have the capacity for DEIJ. From 7–12, education for Feeling; children learn belonging and love for the world. From 12–21, education for Thinking; children recognize difference and identity development.

Educating Children's Will (EC)

Developing the Sense of Touch -- This sense will, in later time, grow into:
- Development of physical and emotional awareness of self and others.
- Development of healthy boundaries, love for self and others.
- Development of a consciousness of freedom.
- Development of a perception of belonging.
- Development of intimate relationships and love for "not I."

Developing the Sense of Life -- This sense will, in later time, grow into:
- Capacity for discerning truth vs caricature.
- Capacity for discerning kindness, respect, and encouragement vs meanness, harmfulness, disrespect.
- Capacity for discerning life giving relationship vs empty/wasted relationship.
- Capacity for discerning collaboration and unity vs isolation and disconnection.
- Capacity for discerning humor vs mockery, sarcasm, or insult.
- Capacity for discerning living (imaginative) knowledge vs dry (intellectual) knowledge.

Developing the Sense of Movement -- This sense will, in later time, grow into:
- Capacity for recognizing, reading, and understanding movements of historical streams.
- Capacity for recognizing, reading, and understanding movements of political streams.
- Capacity for recognizing, reading, and understanding movements of economic streams.
- Capacity for recognizing, reading, and understanding movements of societal streams.
- Capacity for recognizing, reading, and understanding movements of heredity/ancestral streams.
- Capacity for recognizing, reading, and understanding movements of cultural streams.
- Capacity for recognizing, reading, and understanding movements of philosophical and intellectual streams
- Capacity for recognizing, reading, and understanding movements of religious streams.

Developing the Sense of Balance -- This sense will, in later time, grow into:
- Development of experiential wisdom regarding justice.
- Development of experiential wisdom regarding balanced, healthy organizations.
- Development of experiential wisdom regarding balanced, healthy society and systems.
- Development of experiential wisdom regarding balanced, healthy relationships.

Figure 11.

Educating Children's Thinking (EC)

- Creation of a dialogue space for children to share their experience of their home environments.
- Creation of a dialogue space for children to share their cultural experiences.
- Creation of a dialogue space for children to share their observations, questions, and wonderings, when the time is right.

Figure 12.

Educating Children's Feeling (EC)

- Invite traditions, songs, languages, art objects, books, and festivals of families of different cultures
- Create a learning environment for children within the class community.
- Bring visual images, art objects, stories, festivals from other cultures to enrich learning environments.

- Wet on wet watercolor painting experience – merging of different colors (kindergarten), creating a third color.
- Experience singing in unison.
- Experience moving in unison.
- Experience playing together.

Figure 13.

In the last part of the session, we talked about DEIJ in early childhood education, focusing on the educational process in relation to the uniqueness of each child, as well as how the four fundamental senses are going to evolve into a healthy consciousness of DEIJ. I have summed up our discussion in figures 8–13.

Based on our shared observation and workshop participation, we concluded that DEIJ and the liberation of all people are the ultimate goals of Steiner's vision. We resolved to carry this new understanding of Waldorf education forward into our work.

References

Steiner, Rudolf. 1916. "The Ego-Consciousness of the So-Called Dead." GA 168. February 22, Leipzig. See, e.g., *Awakening Anthroposophy in the World.* https://rsarchive.org/Lectures/19160222p01.html.

Examining the Impact of Generational Trauma on Young Black Boys

Lisa Miccio

Recently, a parent in my mixed-age kindergarten class at the Waldorf School of Garden City, New York, shared with me that "Black families are always living in times of uncertainty," and that she and her husband would like for me to please remember that their son is a Black boy carrying inherited trauma from his enslaved ancestors. Soon after this, I was invited to lead a workshop at the 2022 WECAN conference, "Toward a Kinder, More Compassionate Society." My initial response was to ask, "Who am I to think that I can lead a workshop meant to deepen the conference theme of inclusivity, diversity, equity, and access?" However, as I considered the conference subtitle—"Working Together Toward Change"—and reflected on my reading about the impact of generational trauma on young Black boys, I recognized that leading this workshop would be an opportunity for me, a white woman of privilege, to step forward as an ally and a learner willing to share her experience with how we might begin to reconcile Waldorf education's message that "the world is good" with the reality of inherited trauma and its effects on Black boys and men. I could raise awareness about ways that inherited post-traumatic stress disorder (PTSD) can impact the behaviors of Black boys in our Waldorf classrooms and explore steps towards healing their hypervigilance, while also helping to change the distorted narrative that they hear from the world around them.

A Call to Action

I opened the workshop by reflecting on a question that began forming as I prepared for the workshop. Why have I never been asked in a job interview to share any training or experience that prepares me to meet the needs of Black children in the kindergarten? Even at the Waldorf School of Garden City, where ten out of my fourteen children are children of color, I was never asked that question during my interview process. And, while Waldorf teacher training institutions are now implementing coursework to address this, teachers like me, who completed a Waldorf teacher training prior to these curricular additions, have work to do if we hope to meet the crisis moments that are upon us, especially if we hope to teach Black children. This recognition brought to mind the following statement from Rudolf Steiner's lecture "Education in the Face of the Present Day World Situation": "Just think what feelings arise in the soul of the early childhood educator who realizes: what I accomplish with this child, I accomplish for the grown-up person in his twenties. What matters is not so much a knowledge of abstract educational principles or pedagogical rules. . . . [W]hat does matter is that a deep sense of responsibility develops in our hearts and minds and affects our world view and the way we stand in life" (Steiner 1920).

Next, I shared a call to action from diversity advocate Verna Myers in her TED talk, "How to Overcome Our Biases" (2014). Ms. Myers examines her own implicit biases and encourages viewers to recognize their biases in order to actively transform them. After viewing the video, participants were asked to reflect on Ms. Myers's encouragement to begin taking steps to walk towards our own discomfort by journaling their connections to her assertion that "It's not about perfection but about connection" when engaging in DEI (diversity, equity, and inclusion) work.

Introducing Post-Traumatic Slave Syndrome and Inherited Trauma

"History is not the past; it is the present. We carry our history with us. We are our history."

—*James Baldwin,* I Am Not Your Negro

I was somewhat familiar with inherited trauma, but before one of my Black parents mentioned it in relation to her son, I had never thought about it in the context of the work that I do daily with kindergarten children. The idea of intergenerational trauma was in a box with a very dusty lid, up on a very high shelf. But when she shared with me that perhaps the reason her son moves so fast, as if he is driven, is that his ancestors had to produce and work quickly, for fear of being sold, I began reading about generational trauma. In the words of Dr. Joy DeGruy, "Post Traumatic Slave Syndrome is a condition that exists when a population has experienced multigenerational trauma resulting from centuries of slavery and continues to experience oppression and institutionalized racism today." (DeGruy [2005] 2017).

In my workshop, I introduced Dr. DeGruy and her work through a video in which she shares some of the effects of slavery upon Black (and white) people today. In her book, Dr. DeGruy explains that generational trauma can be inherited, that trauma changes a person's DNA and can be passed down. The changes from trauma do not damage the genes, but rather leave a chemical mark that determines how the gene is expressed. This is what is known as an epigenetic change. Epigenetics refers to how certain genes are turned on or off, rather than actual changes in the DNA sequence. Scientists who study epigenetics have found that trauma experienced by parents can impact the DNA and behavior of their offspring for generations to come.

I also introduced Resmaa Menakem's work on racialized trauma as presented in his book *My Grandmother's Hands: Racialized Trauma and the Pathway to Mending Our Hearts and Bodies* (2017), and we reviewed research that documents the effects of racialized trauma and the distorted narratives told about Black men and boys (Color of Change 2015), along with research that reports biases held among preschool teachers in regard to Black boys and girls (ABC Action News 2016). The Yale report's findings help explain why Black students tend to be suspended at much higher rates than white students.

What Can We Do?

For the remainder of the workshop, our attention turned towards how we can make a difference. I shared the following from Sabine Joseph (2020), the founder of All of Us Crayons;

> *Dear my child's future teacher(s):*
> *The absolute best thing you can say to our family at the end of the first school day is: "I just wanted to let you know that I recognize and acknowledge that your daughter is one of the few African American students in the class. I will do my best to be present and aware of the challenges that may present themselves and I will keep a sensitive level of awareness to the activities and conversations amongst her peers that may make her uncomfortable or single her out. I would like you to keep me aware of any issues that may arise or if there is any way we can make this space a more inviting place for you and your family."*

As Waldorf early childhood teachers, we are used to parents coming to us seeking answers. But how often and in what ways do we center the voices of the Black families in our schools? Do we ask them what they need to feel confident that their children are protected and not just corrected?

In the fall of 2021, the DEIJ committee at the Waldorf School of Garden City (New York) did just that by inviting six Black fathers to form a panel to meet with our faculty and staff. Their intention was to help us better understand their Black children and other Black students by seeing who they are in the fullness of their families—to see from whom our Black students have come.

This was a new and revolutionary opportunity in our school. While we have a diverse community of students, and a Black student union in the High School, and while we've been talking about creating affinity groups for parents and younger students, this was the first time we created space for our Black families to share with us their experiences as parents of Black children. It was the first time that we centered the voices of our Black parents. The Black fathers who spoke with our faculty and staff offered a gift, which I shared with my workshop participants. The gift is a list of immediate steps we can all begin taking, and include:

First, take what we say today and bring it back into your classroom and your department meetings.

- Learn about the ways that distorted media messages affect our Black youth.
- Get to know Black boys and their families to better understand what shapes our experiences.
- There is a psychological aspect to what our Black young men and boys experience. Be in tune to this and share it with others.
- Interrupt the distorted narrative being told in our country about who Black boys and Black men are and start a new narrative. Find ways to amplify the voices of Black men and boys in your school.
- Remember that "Kids don't care what you know until they know you care." Develop true and meaningful relationships with Black young men and Black boys by creating space for honest, authentic dialogue.
- Explore whether Black boys are punished more frequently and more harshly in your school and if so—then challenge yourselves to look at the implicit bias at work. Get comfortable calling out bias when you see it in your colleagues, students, and parent community.

In my WECAN workshop, I tried to recreate the essence of what these fathers shared by presenting a video created by the *New York Times* called "A Conversation with My Black Son" (2015).

The workshop concluded with inspiration from Toni Morrison and Dr. Keith Hinderlie. Toni Morrison asks us: "When a child walks in the room, your child or anybody else's child, do your eyes light up? That's what they're looking for" (OWN 2011). And Dr. Hinderlie (2022) suggests that we incorporate the following practices in our work with Black boys:

- "Love Bomb": heap love and affirmations on our Black and Brown students. They need to feel seen, valued and celebrated. And this goes for their parents too. Tell your parents about what a good day their son had and share with them observations of their son so that they know he is being seen.
- Consider implementing a PBIS (Positive Behavioral Interventions Strategy) that includes instituting a four-to-one affirmation to corrections ratio.
- Lastly, he encourages us to front-load support for Black boys. Do not wait until an incident arises, but instead put into place supportive measures like counseling, affinity groups, and mentoring to offset the everyday trauma of being Black in America.

The World Is Good

I continue to work to reconcile my daily message to the children—that the world is good—with my growing awareness of the daily challenges that our communities of color face in our country. According to Dr. DeGruy, being Black in America means living with chronic PTSD caused not only by one's lived experiences, but also by the experiences of one's ancestors. And yet, "the brain is a meaning-making machine, always trying to make sense of the world. If our view of the world is that people are good, then we will anticipate good things from people. We project that expectation in our interactions with others and thereby actually elicit good from them. Our internal view of the world becomes a self-fulfilling prophecy; we project what we expect, and that helps elicit what we expect" (Perry and Winfrey 2021, 51). Therefore, through my own inner work and my devotion to the children in my care, I have come to believe that we can make a difference in shaping our young Black boys' experiences and convey that the world is good through our daily commitment to making their experiences with us truly good. That means understanding the current obstacles in their paths and working as allies to help remove them. That means changing the narrative they experience through the media to the one that we tell every day through relationship and devotion. That means heaping lots of love and affirmations on them daily to counteract the correction that they feel each day from simply being Black in America. Which also means "that a deep sense of responsibility develops in our hearts and minds and affects our world view and the way we stand in life" (Steiner 1920).

References

ABC Action News. Sept. 28, 2016. "New Study by Yale University Suggests Racial Bias Could Be Seen as Early as Preschool." YouTube video. https://youtu.be/tF3A990Koro.

Color of Change. March 2015. *Not to Be Trusted: Dangerous Levels of Inaccuracy in TV Crime Reporting in NYC.* https://s3.amazonaws.com/s3.colorofchange.org/images/ColorOfChangeNewsAccuracyReportCardNYC.pdf.

DeGruy, Joy. (2005) 2017. *Post Traumatic Slave Syndrome: America's Legacy of Enduring Injury & Healing.* Portland, OR: Joy DeGruy Publications, Inc.

Hinderlie, Keith. Feb. 8, 2022. "Educating Boys." Lecture at the conference of the New York State Association of Independent Schools.

Joseph, Sabine (sabbbine). Feb. 11, 2020. "Dear my child's future teacher(s)." Instagram post. https://www.instagram.com/p/B8ba5VthfPz/?igshid=MDJmNzVkMjY%3D.

Myers, Verna. Dec. 15, 2014. "How to Overcome Our Biases? Walk Boldly Toward Them." TED. YouTube video. https://youtu.be/uYyvbgINZkQ.

Menakem, Resmaa. 2017. *My Grandmother's Hands: Racialized Trauma and the Pathway to Mending Our Hearts and Bodies.* Las Vegas, NV. Central Recovery Press.

New York Times. March 17, 2015. "A Conversation with My Black Son." https://www.nytimes.com/video/opinion/100000003575589/a-conversation-with-my-black-son.html.

OWN. Nov 2, 2011. "Does Your Face Light Up?" Toni Morrison interviewed by Oprah Winfrey. YouTube video. https://youtu.be/9Jw0Fu8nhOc.

Perry, Bruce D., and Oprah Winfrey. 2021. *What Happened To You? Conversations on Trauma, Resilience, and Healing.* New York: Flatiron Books

Steiner, Rudolf. June 10, 1920. “Education in the Face of the Present Day World Situation.” Lecture.

Additional Resources

Peck, Raoul. *I Am Not Your Negro.* Documentary film on James Baldwin. Magnolia Pictures, 2016.

Deepening and Transforming Our Work

Movement Toward Tolerance:
Emphasizing the Four Foundational Senses as a Pathway to Healthy Social Life

Nancy Blanning

Our times call us to equally address two critical goals. We are committing ourselves to truly engage in practices of diversity, equity, inclusion, and justice (DEIJ). At the same time, we are committed to considering the gradually unfolding development and consciousness of the young child as we understand it in Waldorf education. Where and when is it our responsibility to explicitly present guidance to cultivate respect and tolerance for diversity? When and how do we hold the space for implicit offerings showing respect, kindness, and generosity through stories, puppetry, and artistic imaginations?

There is also a parallel question. What developmental experiences provide children a foundation upon which all these urgent messages can take hold? What prepares the human being to develop reverence, tolerance, empathy, compassion, and a sense for justice in social life? Child development viewed through the lens of anthroposophy offers an answer.

The first seven years of a child's life is dedicated to growing a strong physical body. This includes building healthy nerve-sense (thinking), rhythmic (feeling), and metabolic-limb (willing) systems. Rudolf Steiner described this in the first pedagogical lecture given in 1907, years before the founding of the first Waldorf school (Steiner 1907). While growth and development continue throughout life, what is developed in these early years provides a critical foundation for the unfolding of capacities and skills, not only physically, but intellectually and socially as well.

In 1919, Steiner extended this picture of the human being in lectures given to the teachers of the first Waldorf school. In describing the human senses (Steiner 1919), in brief, he expands from the traditional five or six senses to a group of twelve—touch, life or /well-being, self-movement, balance, smell, taste, sight, warmth, hearing, word or speech, thought, and sensing the ego of the other human being. In this ordering, touch is listed first with the ego-sensing of the other human being culminating as the highest of the sensing capacities.

These senses can be divided into three groups. The chart below arranges the senses in this ascending order.

Highest / Social / Spiritual Senses

- Ego-sensing—Sensing the humanity and individuality of another; sensing the ego-being of another person
- Thought—recognize that words are sequenced to convey thoughts expressed by other people
- Word / Language / Speech—sensing that sounds, hand movement, or gesture in particular sequences convey meaning. Sense of word takes sound (or hand movement) and gives it meaning
- Hearing—experiencing sound through the mechanism of the ear

Middle / Feeling Senses

- Warmth—sensing external temperature as warmer or cooler in comparison to our own body temperature. Warmth is a transitional sense
- Sight—taking in visual impressions through the eyes; connected to light

- Taste—experiencing sweet, bitter, salty, and sour by taking in substances through the mouth with help of a watery element (saliva)
- Smell—experiencing outer world through airy element in smells, aromas

Foundational / Will Senses

- Balance / Equilibrium—sensing uprightness and body position inrelation to the earth and gravity
- Self-movement / Proprioception—sensing the cooperative movements of one's limbs and coordination, learning body geography
- Life or Well-Being—sensing the health and balance of inner organic life
- Touch—learning boundary between self and world

Through the first four senses of touch, life, self-movement, and balance, we learn about the well-being and position of our own physical bodies and how we relate to the earth's gravity. These are often called the foundational / will senses and are the primary, critical focus areas in our early childhood education for the first seven years of life. These senses are primarily educated through physical movement, as indicated by Steiner over one hundred years ago. The importance of movement is now being acknowledged and confirmed by neurological research. A motto these days could be that "movement builds the brain." What is accomplished in neurological development through movement (especially well-ordered, purposeful movement) and the opportunity to explore the environment in the first seven years prepares the foundation for future cognitive, emotional, and social life.

The second, middle section of senses—smell, taste, sight, and warmth—gives us information about the nature and qualities of things external to ourselves in the world. These senses are described as the middle or feeling senses, as our experiences through these senses often result our liking or disliking (forming sympathy or antipathy) toward what we encounter.

The third section of senses was new in Steiner's time and identifies subtle sensing capacities as our birthright. These can be called the social and even spiritual senses, through which we recognize and come into relationship with other human beings. These senses are the well-known sense of hearing and newly described senses of word or speech, thought, and sensing the I-being or ego of other human beings.

Another important aspect that Rudolf Steiner shared is that the four foundational senses and the four highest, social senses have relationships with one another. In subtle ways these foundational senses, which are all associated with physically identifiable sensory organs, are the bases out of which the subtle realms of sensing other people and relationships in the social realm metamorphose. This is a very important point to be further developed.

In another lecture, Steiner gave characterizations of "soul states" associated with the senses of touch, life, self-movement, and balance (Steiner 1920). These "soul states" open the door to discovering more subtle qualities carried from the foundational senses to the highest senses in this "metamorphosing" relationship. In brief, the senses and the associated soul states are:

Touch—Permeated by the feeling of God; the sense of being "touched" by God

Life—Feeling of comfort

Self-Movement—Feeling of freedom or being free in one's soul

Balance—Inner rest; feeling oneself as Spirit

From these brief indications, other anthroposophical researchers have expanded upon the picturing and understanding of the senses. Prominent among them are Karl König, the founder of the Camphill communities for special needs children and adults, and Henning Köhler, anthroposophical counselor and author of *Working with Anxious, Nervous, and Depressed Children* (2001) and *Difficult Children: There Is No Such Thing* (2003).

In building upon the soul states and his observations of children's mood-dispositions and sensory development, Henning Köhler takes another step toward bridging how the healthy development of the foundational senses prepares the pathway to reverence, tolerance, empathy, and a sense of justice in the social domain.

The senses are complex and deserves deep study. Rudolf Steiner reflected on the senses for decades before he made any public statement about them. What follows here are only brief characterizations of these foundational senses to advance picturing this sensory path to reverence, tolerance, empathy, and justice.

Touch gives us a sense of boundary. It tells where we stop and where the rest of the world begins. Other conventional views of touch say that it is through touch that we explore the world and learn about what lies outside of ourselves. While this is true, this is not the full picture. Steiner emphasizes that touch gives experience of "boundary." Whenever we touch something outside of our body, we also have an inner experience. This inner experience, caused by something exterior, gives the first experience of boundary, of self and not-self, of self and world. It gives an experience of feeling enclosed.

Life is an organic sense. It provides for us with the experience of well-being. We are consciously aware of this sense when we are unwell with a headache or stomachache, or feel overly tired. When all is well in our organic and metabolic life and we are well rested and not under stress, we are quite unaware of this sense. The life sense can also be called the sense of well-being. A healthy life sense helps us feel secure and cared for, knowing that "all is well." We have a sensation of comfort.

Self-movement is not the ability to move. It is rather the inner faculty that senses when we have moved. It is the sense that helps us to perceive the position of our body parts. Through this sense, we develop body geography and understand how the body is organized. Self-movement allows us to know where the different body parts are in space and in relationship to other body parts without needing to see or to touch them. The sensory organs for self-movement are tiny receptors in the joints, called proprioceptors, that experience the pressure, tension, and angle and position of our limbs. This information is sent to the brain and informs us of body position. This sense is now recognized and confirmed by mainstream research as well.

Balance gives us our experience of uprightness. It informs us, on the one hand, of where the body is in relation to the earth and the force of gravity. The ampulla at the bottom of the inner ear senses this relationship. Another part of the sensory organ for balance is composed of the three semicircular canals within the inner ear. We must have accurate and consistent information from this sensory system to maintain our uprightness and feel secure in standing and moving on the earth. To achieve and maintain uprightness, the human being must have experience of living and moving in the three planes of space—above/below, forward/back, and right/left. The semicircular canals are themselves arranged in these directions and are like miniscule sensory compasses that inform us of where we are in space in relation to these directional pairs.

We usually have a dim consciousness of these lower senses unless something goes wrong through illness or injury. Stiff muscles, for example, can make us more aware of the limbs and their movement and position. Balance awareness is negatively affected by motion sickness.

Each of these senses has characteristic experiences that help build healthy strength in its domain.

Touch is made whole by many, many different touch experiences of texture, shape, density, size, roughness, smoothness, prickliness, squishiness, density, and so on. Exploring a great variety of touch sensations confirms that experiences are different, not good or bad. Children in our groups have daily encounters with natural materials, practical work, cooking, and exploring the natural world outdoors. Warm and comfortable clothing assure children that they have an enclosing, safe boundary around their skin. Gentle, secure, appropriate touching in the infant and toddler years is the most essential experience for young children to gain security from touch—to subtly know that they are "touched by God" (see, e.g., Köhler 2001, 46-48). Another word we can use to describe being "touched" or "held" by God is trust.

Life / Well-being is nourished by regular rhythms, routine, and predictability in the child's care. Babies may cry frantically when cold, wet, or hungry. But when response comes reliably from a warm and loving caregiver, the baby begins to develop a "positive peacefulness." While gratification may not come immediately, the child learns that care will come and can be relied upon. Little by little, the child can tolerate delay in gratification in incremental stretches. A well-tended life sense "gives growing children the agreeable sensation of inner restfulness and the security of self-containment . . . of being sheltered and stable" (Köhler 2001, 27-29). One feels comfortable in one's being.

Köhler goes on to describe how loving care provided in this way, coupled with the example of peacefulness and patience demonstrated by those around them and the support of spiritual forces carried by the child's angel provide the groundwork for developing tolerance in moral and social life.

In speaking of tolerance, Köhler states: "It is possible to listen to and understand others in their individual difference, to accept them as they are, and take real interest in them, only if we stand firmly on our own ground while meeting them with inner collectedness and circumspection of a confident life sense orientation that has been built into our personality structure [which shows itself as a certain degree of selflessness.] We can forget ourselves only when we are firmly self-grounded; otherwise, self-forgetting begets fear, fear that [creates a hurried and intolerant mood], seeking refuge in our accustomed opinions and prejudices, sympathies, and antipathies" (Köhler 2001, 38).

"Active tolerance" is the goal. "Active tolerance means not only leaving others free to be themselves in all their individual differences, while taking a gentle and unprejudiced interest in them, but really wanting to understand them sufficiently to honor their ways of being and behaving without judging by one's own standard" (Köhler 2001, 39).

The predictable rhythmic routines and schedules of our days, weeks, and yearly festival celebrations provide strong support to a healthy life sense. Nourishing foods; natural materials; clothing appropriate to the season; carefully chosen colors to nourish and not shock the senses; and a warm, friendly, inviting mood in the classroom support the life sense on a daily basis. The more we more consciously carry the power and importance of these reassuring rhythms, the more powerful they become in supporting the children.

Self-movement finds its joyous expression in movement of the limbs. Self-movement educates itself by feeling the position of and pressure within the joints of the limbs. Whenever we push, pull, hang, lift, jump, stomp, hold our body weight on our hands and arms, wring water out of a towel, stir a thick batter, chop vegetables, knead a big portion of bread dough, hammer, saw, rasp, shovel, carry heavy objects, climb, and so on, we are supporting healthy self-movement. This sense is only educated through physical movement. Through self-movement we acquire body geography. The more the body moves in repeated, purposeful sequences, the more coordination and control the child acquires. In other words, the body does what the child wishes it to do "with 'a dreamlike sureness'" (Köhler 2001, 84-85). Having this capacity "is what gives us, even in seemingly hopeless situations, the confidence to summon up a new impulse to move on in life, to change direction, to develop initiative" (Köhler 2001, 86). We have the perception of being free in our own mobility. Steiner's connection of self-movement with "being a free spirit" captures this.

On a soul or social level, what does this capacity transform to? "When we have some gripping experience, we speak of it as 'moving.' What is being moved? It is the inner human being . . . Our ability to perceive our own inner stirrings also enables us to understand and participate in the soul stirrings of others" (Köhler 2001, 87). If we imagine this further as the child matures, being able to move into the inner experience of the other is the beginning of empathy and compassion, soul virtues sorely needed in our troubled and divisive times. Whenever we give the children opportunity for meaningful, sequential movement in circle imaginations, ring games, purposeful work, and all the things named above, we are paving the path toward social empathy and compassion.

Balance is the companion and complementary partner of self-movement. Henning Kohler states: "Our whole feeling of being at ease, our whole capacity for coordination, would be as good as useless if we were unable to keep our balance. In every sequence of movements, in every moment of just standing upright, Balance has to be continuously maintained" (Kohler 2001, 107). But while the body is in movement, Balance provides the sense of inner quiet. With this inner quiet, the human being is always the same self no matter what time, space, or position the body is in. Steiner says that it is a sensing of oneself as spirit.

How is balance educated in the physical body? As with its partner self-movement, balance is also strengthened and matured through movement. Balance loves all movements that circle and spin, swing, twirl, rock, bend, sway/nod/rotate the head, and climb. Balance thrives on its practice through walking on beams, logs, wiggling rocks, uneven ground, and so on. As the body and balancing or vestibular systems go through all these gyrations, the "inner quiet" practices keeping itself steady.

The word "balance" brings forth another picture, too—the old-fashioned scales with weighing pans on either side to sense the relative weight of what one side holds in comparison to the other. We can balance our body physically to find a centered stance. When things are out of balance, we can readjust to recreate equilibrium through movement of body position. In the soul realm, this physical balancing becomes the capacity for judgment. "Making judgments means arriving at an outlook that resolves or rises above a problem, a process in which what at first seems insoluable is brought into harmonious accord. . . We try to restore symmetry in our thinking and feeling." This is what we know as a sense of justice. "The sense of justice is simply a sublimation of the sense of balance coupled with the capacity for empathy transmitted by the sense of motion. Fellow feeling and compassion are indissolubly bound up . . . with the sense of justice. Far from a moral standpoint, a feeling for justice is feeling for symmetry, an inner impulse to bring restitution in restoring human dignity where it has suffered" (Kohler 2001, 115).

These descriptions provide a more complete picture of each foundational sense and what capacities—trust, tolerance, empathy/compassion, and justice—healthy development supports. The next step is to return to Rudolf Steiner's insight that the four foundational and four highest, social senses stand in paired relationship to one another.

- Touch is related to sensing the I-being of the other
- Life/well-being is related to sensing the thought of another
- Self-movement is related to moving with the word or speech of another
- Balance is related to the capacity for hearing

A healthy **touch** sense provides experience of boundary. I am secure in myself and can approach another person with trust, sensing where I stop and the other person begins. Security from my physical touch rises to the social sphere in sensing the I-being of the other; I can trust our sameness and not be fearful or anxious of the other person's differences from me.

A healthy **life** sense provides a sense of well-being that supports development of tolerance. Other thoughts, attitdes, cultural experiences, religious orientations, gender expressions, and racial identites may be different from mine. Yet I can feel secure and comfortable in my own being through well-nourished touch and reliable life rhythms. I can not only tolerate this diversity but find it interesting.

Self-movement affects both our outward physical and inward social or emotional movements. My physical body knows how to move with coordination through self-movement. Through self-movement turned inward, I can do this within myself and I can also move inwardly with others, sensing how an experience may feel for them. This capacity opens the door to empathy and compassion with others. Through my feeling, I can sense my way into another's inner life in a respectful and tender way.

Balance provides an experience of equanimity, of symmetrical, even-tempered equilibrium of the physical body through finding a centered point of intersection in the three planes of space. Steiner described balance as affording an "inner rest." In order to elevate my hearing to listening, I must find the inner quiet that allows me to encounter the words, feelings, actions, and thoughts of the others. I sense my way to achieving an inner balance of what I observe. This expresses itself outwardly as a sense of justice. What I sense inwardly as a balanced and fair view, I can project outwardly into the social world in which we all live.

The physical and neurological development of the senses creates the foundation upon which important non-visible intellectual, emotional, and social capacities can grow. Attention to supporting the sense of touch, life or well-being, self-movement, and balance is foundational. In our times, this support is essential to the future years of growing, thinking, feeling, and willing as a full human being.

There are explicit DEIJ messages that we must stand for with bravery and moral integrity. And children also need a chance to dream into imaginations where they see themselves as being recognized, cared for, and safe and sheltered. Their souls crave to know that goodness is always present, even when we cannot see it.

For all of this to take root and flourish, children equally need dedicated support to grow robust, secure, reliable grounding in the four foundational senses as the preparation for the more compassionate, kind, and just world we all working together to manifest.

References

Köhler, Henning. 2001. *Working with Anxious, Nervous, and Depressed Children*. Fair Oaks, CA: Association of Waldorf Schools of North America.

———. 2003. *Difficult Children: There Is No Such Thing*. Fair Oaks, CA: Association of Waldorf Schools of North America.

Steiner, R. 1907. *The Education of the Child in the Light of Spiritual Science*. Great Barrington, MA: Anthroposophic Press.

———. 1919. Lecture 8, *Study of Man*. London: Rudolf Steiner Press.

———. 1920. "Man's Twelve Senses in Their Relation to Imagination, Inspiration, and Intuition." Lecture given in Dornach, Switzerland, August 8, 1920.

Additional Resources

Aeppli, Willi. *Care and Development of the Human Senses*. Translated by Valerie Freilich. Edinburgh, UK: Floris Books, 2013.

Schoorel, Edmond. *The First Seven Years: The Physiology of Childhood*. Fair Oaks, CA: Rudolf Steiner College Press, 2004.

Wiehl, Angelika, and Wolfgang-Michael Auer, eds. *Understanding Child Development: Steiner's Essential Principles for Waldorf Education*. Spring Valley, NY: Waldorf Early Childhood Association of North America, 2020.

Beautiful Me, Beautiful You

Melody Birdsong-Shubert

It is an absolute human certainty that no one can know [their] own beauty or perceive a sense of [their] own worth until it has been reflected back to [them] in the mirror of another loving, caring human being.

—John Joseph Powell, Loyola University

My early childhood and young adulthood were fraught with the dogma that religion sometimes incites. People making life choices that differed from those accepted within the organization my family belonged to were officially excluded from social engagement. I felt conditionally loved and not at all seen. Life as a young, Black adult outside of the religious realm and my interracial family unit revealed the reality that, as a human being in this world, the sense of worth held by my white counterparts was not applicable to me. Nor was it applicable to other members of society who were systematically oppressed.

My experience as a Waldorf teacher became an unfortunate déjá vu of my experiences as a Black person in society. As a supporting teacher, I had been in awe of the magical yellow-brick road of daily rhythms paved by a skilled teacher. But as a Black person, I longed for my colleagues to trade in their rose-colored glasses for antibias lenses. As it happened, the lead teacher with whom I worked longed for the opportunities awaiting them outside the classroom walls. After their departure was announced, the transition for me to lead the last eight weeks of the school year proceeded with ease and grace within the established framework of the community. It wasn't until the following year, when an expanded class community was introduced, that the deep, intentional work required to incorporate diversity was truly recognized. And it became apparent that a whole other skill set was required to create a classroom environment where the practice of cultural humility lived when it was not practiced in the educational institution as a whole.

But it is the task of Waldorf educators to expand our lens, continually practice being antibias, anti-racist (ABAR) educators and to consciously play a key role in forming a compassionate and just society. The work of an ABAR educator is a never-ending wrestle that continually unfolds. Looking deeply into how one wants to express humanness and what qualities one wishes to bestow as an educator is an essential part of the process.

There are many organizations providing support through incredible resources and educational and networking opportunities. The National Association for the Education of Young Children (NAEYC) provided resounding foundational support for my work. Their book, *Anti-bias Education for Young Children and Ourselves* (Derman-Sparks and Edwards 2010), set the stage for reflection and the opportunity to delve more deeply into the work, giving me more knowledge and the confidence to grow. And, because this work can only progress to the span of one's current perception, continued reflection, education, and collaboration are all necessary.

Every human being has a personal identity. NAEYC defines *personal identity* as "attributes that give each person a sense of individuality. Includes factors such as a person's first name, personality, talents, interests, age, and the specifics of and relationships with family members. Primarily fostered by a child's temperament, home, and extended family, and then by community and school experiences." This personal assessment of oneself is largely unaffected by others. Every human being also has a social identity. The National Association for the Education of Young Children defines *social identity* as "assigned memberships in groups defined by the society and shared with many other people. Identities include economic class, gendered identity, heritage, racialized identity, and religion. Each of these social identities is connected to societal advantages and disadvantages" (Derman-Sparks and Edwards 2010, chapter 2). We all juggle the implications of social identity bias that lives within us, our schools, and extended communities.

A narrative poem by New Jersey poet Lew Gardner (1973)was included in "Curriculum As Window and Mirror" by Emily Style ([1988] 1996, 2). The poem and points that follow vividly detail the harm that results from prejudice-centered social identity concepts.

My mother's uncle had a horse.
The best time of a deadly relatives' Sunday
was to walk with him to the stable
and watch him feed the quiet animal,
to give it sugar from my own hand
and jump back away
from the big warm tongue,
to smell the hay and manure, to see
the white horse in the next stall,
with tail and mane like yellow silk.

If my mother and I ran into him
as he and the horse were making their rounds,
buying up the wonderful junk
they heaped and hauled in the wagon,
he'd lift me up to the seat
and let me hold the reins and yell "Giddy-up!"

In the spring of 4th grade,
one afternoon of silent division
we heard a clanking and looked outside.

My great-uncle! I could tell them all
how I had held those reins!
But everyone laughed at the hunched old man,
the obsolete wagon and horse,
the silly, clattering junk.
I did not tell them.

Style (1988, 3) goes on to say:

> *While everyone in that fourth grade classroom looks out the same window, they do not all see the same old man. For all but one, their knowledge is "detached" and "objective." And all but one of them suffer (unaware) from the limitation of their detachment. The poem's narrator, on the other hand, is aware of his suffering as he acquires another view of the old man to whom he is intimately connected. Prior to the classroom window experience, the narrator's view had been purely provincial. Now he is forcefully educated during "one afternoon of silent division" to see more than he has before. He sees his great-uncle reduced to being a mere "Other" in the eyes of the others. But there are more observations to be gleaned from this poetic incident. The child's (understandable) silence means that the others in the classroom remain trapped in their limited, "objective" view of the old man. His otherness, his alien nature, is all they can see.*

As early childhood educators, we know that young children make sense of the world through observation. Their observations are formulated into ideas and feelings that can be pre-prejudice. The hugely negative impact occurs when these pre-prejudice ideas and feelings are not interrupted. These ideas and feelings can develop into real prejudice when the adults around them choose inaction. Allowing these ideas and feelings to settle in and take hold unaddressed makes space for them becoming their perceived reality. It is our responsibility to foster a healthy identity and promote caring connections and an appreciation of differences.

An educational institution should strive to be restorative in nature. This is best achieved through full community participation and agreement on what it means to be an affirming, antibias, anti-racist institution. Below are some strategies to begin blueprinting this community effort once the meaning behind it has been established.

- Have your school make a public verbal and written confirmation of their commitment to practice being an affirming, antibias, anti-racist community that holds itself accountable. This could take place at an all-school event like a back-to-school affair and also be stated on the school website's homepage and social media profiles.
- Open houses, tours, admissions process, and employee interviews should all hold space to clearly communicate the practices to which the institution holds its community accountable.
- Put your employee biography on your school's website and consider whether it reflects your ABAR values and intentions.

Continue your dedication to self-reflection, education, and collaboration with class communities. This will strengthen and nurture the positive identities of our students, their families, and ourselves. And it lays the groundwork for comfort with and awareness of the value of diversity within each class and the school community as a whole. Here are some strategies:

- Welcome letters and class meetings provide an opportunity to clearly articulate your ABAR values and intentions and the expectation that parents partner with you.
- Discover the core values and pleasure goals of your class community.
- Share in reflection activities during class meetings. The template for the "Where I Am From" poem (AUX Sable Middle School N.d.) could initiate thought invoking adult discussion.

- Encourage parents/guardians to share golden moments and their children's tender spots.
- Invite parents/guardians into your classroom, resist the urge to micromanage and trust they will add richness to your days.

Intentionally nurturing positive social identities using an ABAR lens can be organically woven into the Waldorf early childhood curriculum. Books and storytelling can be remarkable tools when utilized as an introductory stepping stone into the world of another and as a reflection of self. Here are some ideas to get you started:

- Research the content, delivery, and authorship, and seek to understand the benefits of a chosen tale.
- Be conscious of what each story brings to the children. Was Peter Rabbit "very naughty"? Or, like his siblings, was Peter also a good little bunny who made a naughty choice?
- Incorporate the reading of picture books into class rhythms.
- Bridge the partnership between home and school with a classroom borrowing library which contains wholesome books that support child development as well as antibias and anti-racist strivings.
- Share tips with parents for choosing these types of stories and welcome recommendations and donations from the children's families. Learning for Justice provides "A Tool for Selecting Diverse Texts" (2016) that supports both novices and those proficient at selecting books to help shape curriculum and home experience.

Being an ABAR educator requires taking and creating the opportunities in our daily interactions. We must reflect on ways to create a space of windows and mirrors in order to challenge bias proactively as opportunities arise. And, opportunities, whether taken or missed, require our reflection. When considering the choices we make to shape our class community in support of healthy identity, we can ask: Did this resist or reinforce the prejudice within societal constructs?

Consider the many social identities of each of your students and families. Categorize them into a table according to societal constructs.

- Would this social identity be classified as an advantage or disadvantage?
- How will you proactively support pride and appreciation for this aspect of the child's identity?
- What classroom experiences will encourage resistance to the societal construct of this aspect of their identity?

I had the fortunate opportunity of participating in a Lifeways course where Cynthia Aldinger shared an experience of an early childhood conference she attended in Toronto at which Fred Rogers of *Mr. Rogers' Neighborhood* was the keynote speaker. He stood before the audience and said, "You know, when you stand before another human being, you are standing in sacred space." Let us live by these words as we lay the groundwork for comfort with and appreciation of the value of diversity within our classes and school communities.

All good wishes on your work!

References

AUX Sable Middle School. N.d. "Where I From Poem." http://asms.psd202.org/documents/jrossi/1510234129.pdf. Accessed September 8, 2022. See the template and original poem on 4–5.

Derman-Sparks, Louise, and Julie Olsen Edwards. 2010. *Anti-Bias Education for Young Children and Ourselves*. Washington, DC: National Association for the Education of Young Children.

Gardner, Lew. 1973. "My mother's uncle had a horse." In "Curriculum as Window and Mirror" by Emily Style (1988) 1996.

Learning for Justice. 2016. "A Tool for Selecting Diverse Texts." https://www.learningforjustice.org/sites/default/files/general/Reading%20Diversity%20Lite%E2%80%94Teacher%27s%20Edition2.pdf. Accessed September 1, 2022.

Style, Emily. (1988) 1996. "Curriculum as Window and Mirror." *Social Science Record* (Fall). http://www.nationalseedproject.org/images/documents/Curriculum_As_Window_and_Mirror.pdf. Accessed September 1, 2022.

Additional Resources

Powell, John Joseph. *The Secret of Staying in Love.* Allen, TX: Thomas More Pub. Co., 1974.

Project Implicit. https://implicit.harvard.edu/implicit/takeatouchtest.html. Accessed September 8, 2022.

Not Just Meaning Well, But Doing Well

Sondi Eugene

We began with giving workshop participants a chance to update their name and pronouns in the Zoom interface. Once all of the participants were in the session, everyone had a chance to introduce themselves with their name, school affiliation (if any), and their years teaching or being involved with diversity work.

The session then "officially" began with the America Verse—"May our feeling penetrate into the center of our heart. And seek in love, to unite itself with the human beings seeking the same goal. With the spirit beings who, bearing grace, strengthening us from realms of light, and illuminating our love, are gazing down upon our earnest, heartfelt, striving" (Steiner 1923).

Active Listening

We strove for the following during our discussion:

- To be mindful of creating space for people of color, their voices and experiences
- To assume positive intent and to take responsibility for the impact of our words

- To stay fully present—especially during Zoom sessions
- To encourage and give appreciation when others are sharing
- To observe confidentiality

Inner Work

We explored our own biographies to see how our experiences might be helping or hindering our work with concepts of inclusion, diversity, equity, and access. We asked ourselves: How do I show up as a teacher and colleague?

Power Flower Exercise

Everyone has multiple, nuanced identities that form our lives. Gender, race, ethnicity, age, education—it's how these intersect and interact that shape who we are and what challenges and contradictions we confront, and hopefully gives us a fuller understanding of intersectionality that helps us become more integrated and sensitive human beings.

The power flower exercise explores our intersecting identities and the ways that they contribute to both oppression and privilege. We can experience oppression and privilege simultaneously. Power is relational and always dynamic. By reflecting on how these forces operate in people's lives, we deepen our understanding of how identity, power, and exclusion affect our schools, faculty, parents, and ourselves as individuals. We reflected on our experiences with the following, guided by a quote widely attributed to Malcolm X: "We need more light about each other. Light creates understanding, understanding creates love, love creates patience, and patience creates unity."

- Race
- Sex
- Sexual orientation
- Ability/disability
- Social class
- Language

- Education level
- Age group

Each participant made their own flower power drawing. We discussed who represented the dominant group for each of these categories, and then each person colored their flower as they wished, showing the intersecting areas and surprises. After drawing, we shared our discoveries with a partner.

Racial Awareness (1)

Each participant journaled for ten minutes about the following questions and then shared with a partner. We reflected on Isabel Wilkerson's words (2020): "Radical empathy means putting in the work to educate oneself and to listen with a humble heart to understand another's experience from their perspective, not as we imagine what we would feel. It is the kindred connection from a place of deep knowing that opens your spirit to the pain of another as they perceive it."

- What is your earliest memory of noticing that people have different skin color, eye shapes, hair texture and color? What was your first significant encounter with someone who looked "different" from you/your family?
- When did you first begin to think about yourself as having racial identity? What name did you put on your racial identity? How did you feel about your racial identity then? If you did not think about this as a child, why do you think that was?

Debate Vs. Dialogue (Dogs and Cats)

Debate is a form of communication between two or more people where an issue is discussed and opposing arguments are put forth. It further:

- Assumes there is one right answer and that you have it;
- Is about proving someone else is wrong;
- Is about listening to find flaws and weaknesses in other people's ideas;
- The goal of debate is to win.

Dialogue is a form of communication between two or more people that is directed toward common understanding. It further:

- Assumes many people have the answer and that only together can find the solution;
- Is collaborative, with participants work together toward a common understanding;
- Is about learning through listening to others and discovering new ideas;
- The goal of dialogue is to understand.

Partners had a chance to "try out" both dialogue and debate, guided by words widely attributed to Maya Angelou: "In diversity there is beauty and there is strength."

Racial Awareness (2)

We journaled for ten minutes about the following questions and then shared with our partners. We were guided by Nelson Mandela's words (1995): "No one is born hating another person because of the color of his skin, or his background, or his religion. People must learn to hate, and if they can learn to hate, they can be taught to love, for love comes more naturally to the human heart than its opposite."

- Where and when (describe the situation) did you first hear a racial epithet?
- What is an early memory of realizing that some people are treated differently (better or worse) because of their racial identity?

Zones

We all have zones of comfort when having difficult conversations and doing social justice work often asks us to move beyond our traditional areas of comfort so that we can open ourselves to new challenges, knowledge, and awareness. Inside our comfort zone we are rarely being challenged, therefore rarely learning.

We call the edge of our comfort zone the growth or learning zone. When we are on the growth/learning edge, we are most open to expanding our knowledge and understanding as well as expanding our comfort zone itself. Being on this edge can be uncomfortable or we may feel out of balance. We may experience this as feeling annoyed, angry, anxious, surprised, confused, defensive, or in some other way uncomfortable. These reactions are a natural part of the process of expanding our comfort zone and are a part of the learning process. The challenge is to recognize when we are on a learning edge and then to remain there, and sit with the discomfort we are experiencing, to see what we can learn.

Too far outside of our comfort zone and we begin to resist new information and withdraw. This is the danger zone. We can shut down or have other strong reactions that make it hard or impossible to comprehend new information.

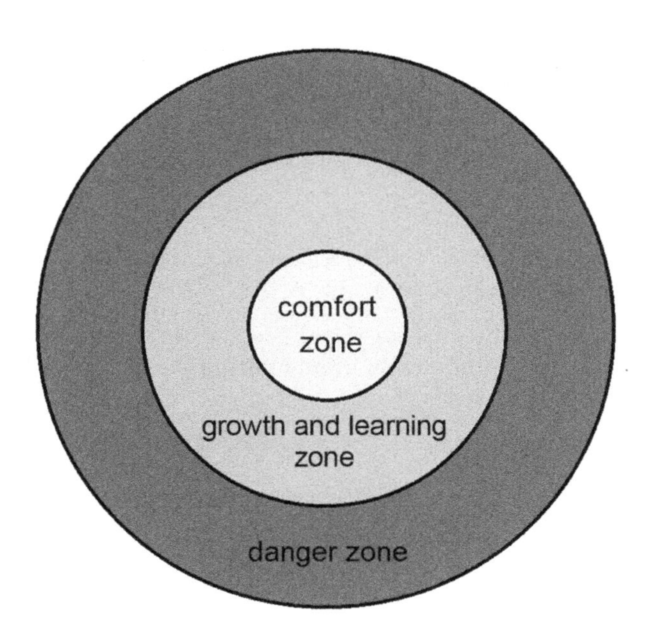

Where are your comfort, growth, and danger zones?

Image courtesy of Wikimedia Commons. Revised with permission.

Racial Awareness (3)

We journaled for ten minutes about the following questions, then shared with our partners. We were guided by the following words, widely attributed to Mahatma Ghandi: "Our ability to reach unity in diversity will be the beauty and the test of our civilization."

- When did you first have any information about people doing something to address racism? How did that affect you?
- What was the most significant image or encounter that you've had regarding race and how has it affected your beliefs, actions and decisions going forward?

Final Sharing

We recognized the role our biographies play in our communication with colleagues, parents, and students; in how we react; or perhaps in how we don't react.

We set two intentions: Don't be afraid to have difficult conversations; and come to these conversations with an open heart and mind.

References

Mandela, Nelson. 1995. *Long Walk to Freedom: The Autobiography of Nelson Mandela.* New York: Back Bay Books.

Steiner, Rudolf. 1923. "The America Verse." See, e.g., the Christian Community website. https://www.thechristiancommunity.org/uncategorized/the-america-verse/. Accessed September 6, 2022.

Wilkerson, Isabel. 2020. *Caste: The Origins of Our Discontents.* New York: Random House.

Weaving Threads of Connection and Inclusion: *Hearts, Gestures, and Hands*

Lynn Turner and Leslie Woolverton-Wetzonis, WECAN I.D.E.A. Coordinators

> *As the tree does not end at the edge of her roots or branches; as the bird does not end at her feathers or with her winged flight; as the earth does not end at her highest mountain, so I do not end at my arm, my foot, my skin.*
>
> —*Cherokee proverb*

How do we consciously integrate inclusive, diverse, equitable and accessible teaching practices that will strengthen our work when we are working primarily within a homogeneous population in our Waldorf community? What does a culturally responsive and equitable Waldorf early childhood classroom look like to you in your parent-child, nursery, and mixed-age kindergarten programs? Our workshop helped to explore what social and emotional building blocks cultivate healthy and thriving child development for *all* children within our Waldorf EC communities. We might be guided by Maya Angelou (2011, 2): "You are the sum total of everything you've ever seen, heard, eaten, smelled, been told, forgot—it's all there. Everything influences each of us."

Inner Development of the Teacher through the Cultivation of Warmth Using an Antibias Lens

We are all being called to teach beyond what we know and who we are. Our inner striving allows us to seek the courage to expand, deepen our knowledge, and widen our lens in our work in the classrooms. Seeing clearly beyond our limited perspectives and intersections allows us to also see past our blind spots. In order to do this, we first need to be able to identify our blind spots, or come to understand our triggers related to race and racism, the unconscious and conscious biases that live within each one of us. When you look at it this way, it becomes very clear—At the heart of this work is "you."

You are the key to this transformative work, and this journey of inner awakening is lifelong. The first action step is to truly see yourself with clear sight. As Rudolf Steiner (1908) said, "Know thyself!" Awakening to see and experience your privilege, bias, and intersectional identity is the essential and foundational step. We can only teach who we are and what we know, so unpacking our blind spots will help us expand our view, empathy, and compassion toward ourselves and others. In our workshop, we offered the following heart meditation verse based on Rudolf Steiner's "The Ensouled Sun of Man" (1924). We asked participants to close their eyes and meditate or reflect on this both individually and as a group.

> *Center your attention in your heart. Imagine there is a small, transparent globe at the center of your heart. Then slowly expand this globe, allowing it to widen through your body, the room, and onward out and out. Keep its shape as it expands through and around the Earth. Let it expand slowly beyond the Earth, through each planetary orbit: Moon, Mercury, Venus, Sun, and farther to the outer planets until it reaches the fixed stars of the Zodiac. Let it rest there, feeling "Held" by the periphery and the powers that stream from it towards the Earth. Then, slowly, contract this globe again, so it passes back through all the spheres, until it is within your own heart again.*

Seeing Bias in a Circle-Drawing Exercise

Our artistic activities helped us all move toward expanding our lens for inclusion while centering love and warmth. We asked our participants to reflect on and incorporate the work from our afternoon together and their own individual life experiences, in order to create circles of identity, of comfort, and of discomfort. In this exercise, we can begin to see what including others can look like. Artistically, this work reveals our own biases. The addition of colors of choice to our identity circles led us toward new discoveries that expressed biases we hadn't been aware of previously.

We all found, by choosing our own colors, that participants could draw an inner circle and discover what is at the center and what is in the periphery of our own lives. How can you center and bring warmth to what is in the periphery? Seeing, naming, and accepting your blind spots is the first step in healing and transformation. This experience was very deepening for all of our participants. It paved the way for further, deeper, dialogue that allowed us greater vulnerability. Discovery within our group and for ourselves individually was profound. Seeing those that we have harmed or impacted negatively by our bias was painful, and we acknowledged this individually and collectively. The artistic experience offered a healing gesture for repair and reconciliation, a starting point for a path forward.

Positive Self-Identity and Healthy Social-Emotional Development through the Art of Puppetry and Storytelling

Supporting the cultivation of positive racial self-identities for all children in the formative years of early childhood from infancy to seven is essential. Now is the time to create mindful, conscious teaching practices that nurture empathy, care of the other, and connection, while supporting the social and emotional wellness of the youngest children. To cultivate this, we need to make cultural and racial connections through honoring and celebrating diversity, especially when none is visible in a community.

Representation matters. All children must see the diversity living in the human population, and storytelling and puppetry provide a wonderful opening to present such diversity. Fairy tales and storytelling are a crucial component of our work. Explore tales from other cultures to share in your classrooms. This adds truth to our storytelling. We're not throwing away what we have used in the past; instead, we are making it richer and more diverse. During the workshop, we shared an example of how we created a diverse living picture of "Sweet Porridge" by the Brothers Grimm (1972, tale 103) to share with young children.

Here are the questions we carried as we sought to create a culturally responsive inner picture and outward imagination for the child:

- What are the racial identities of the puppets in the story? What is the racial representation being centered?
- Do I have Black, Indigenous, or people of color represented? Which archetypes are they representing?
- How will I meet the question of gender bias? Where can I switch roles or otherwise mix the story up to illuminate different perspectives and power centers? To do this we need to bring awareness to the eight social (socially constructed) identifiers: race, ethnicity, sexual orientation, gender identity, ability, religion/spirituality, nationality, and socioeconomic status.
- How am I centering cultural appreciation? Really explore this question. Consider how it might feel to a person from another culture or ethnicity, even when you act with good intentions. Consider whether you are culturally appropriating and cherry-picking content that "fits our/your needs." Grappling with the question of appropriation versus appreciation is necessary. Check in with yourself—how do you feel about the content? If it feels uncomfortable in any way, research the history of the culture being represented, using the eight social identifiers as your guide.

Culturally Responsive and Antibias Parent Education and Communications

Throughout our time together, we reflected and shared stories of how we can begin intentional conversations with parents and with each other (colleagues, faculty, administrators, and school boards) in our work within inclusion, diversity, equity, and access (IDEA) This is both hard work and heart work. It can open wounds and conflicts regarding current questions today but should not be avoided. Rather, we should embrace such work with curiosity, courage, and open hearts.

Some questions that came forward from participants were:

- How can we carry this work forward when we encounter inner resistance from other colleagues, within our schools, and each other? We must ask ourselves to look deeply to uncover what is at the root of the resistance. Is sympathy, antipathy, or both present? Our inner striving must center conscious teaching practices that support and strengthen diversity, equity, inclusion, and access for all. And we have come to see that empathy within our work is the balance that centers this ongoing work.
- How do we meet the barriers of fear and privilege? We must step into our will and take courage as we encounter any and all pushback within ourselves and in others. We need to begin to imagine the possibilities of working from a place of abundance and know that it's all right to experience discomfort as we stretch and grow in our thinking, feeling, and willing. This is hard. Find your peace and maintain your balance.
- How can we weave these threads of inclusion, diversity, equity, and access into our work with children, parents, and colleagues? Understanding what shapes us and our identities is key. We must embrace ourselves as we are and learn to expand out of our comfort zone and into the growth zone if we are to reimagine the work in our classrooms and with our families. This is also especially true in teacher trainings.

- How can we incorporate these concepts in our work in the classroom and with parent education to build a bridge toward a more inclusive, equitable, and kind community? By learning and incorporating culturally responsive antibias language and shared community agreements into parent and school-wide communications, this work will begin to be much more anchored in the everyday life of the school and classroom environment. Begin to reflect on how you can create culturally responsive communications to families and engage in a self-audit of your classroom and interactions with parents, colleagues, and the wider community beyond WECAN.

A concluding note: Continue to explore further the culturally responsive teaching that was shared during the 2022 WECAN conference weekend, summarized in this publication. Continue to hold the inspirational words of our keynote speakers, Keelah Helwig, Meggan Gill, and Joaquin Muñoz. All that was shared throughout the entire 2022 WECAN conference supports social and emotional wellness in all of our work together. Pushback may still occur, but hold onto your center and know that this work celebrates all in the world and certainly our Waldorf community. All of our work within inclusion, diversity, equity and access will carry Waldorf education beyond another one hundred years.

References

Angelou, Maya. April 2011. "Maya Angelou on How to Write—and How to Live." Oprah.com. https://www.oprah.com/spirit/how-to-write-a-poem-maya-angelous-advice. The quote is on the second page of the article, https://www.oprah.com/spirit/how-to-write-a-poem-maya-angelous-advice/2.

Grimm, Jacob and Wilhelm. 1972. *The Complete Grimm's Fairy Tales.* New York: Pantheon Books.

Steiner, Rudolf. Nov. 23, 1908. *What Is Self Knowledge?* GA 108. Lecture given in Berlin, Germany. Awakening Anthropsophy in the World. https://rsarchive.org/Lectures/WS1875_index.html.

———. 1924. "The Ensouled Sun of Man." See, e.g., the Ita Wegman Institute for Fundamental Research into Anthroposophy, Annual Review 2007 (unpublished), 21. https://pdfslide.net/documents/ita-wegman-institute-is-preparing-a-study-edition-of-dr-knigs-3rd-case.html.

Additional Resources

"As the tree does not end . . ." Cherokee proverb shared among Leslie Wetzonis Woolverton's family.

Blue Deer and the Cycle of the Year

Jaime Nuñez-Plata

Introduction

The interest in bringing native cultures from all corners of the world closer to anthroposophy is genuine and requires great commitment. It is not just a matter of celebrating a day or a month, singing a song, or telling a story; it is essential to deeply explore and strive to understand the archetypes that these cultures represent in their symbolism in order to match them with anthroposophy's concepts about the image of man, the earth, and the universe.

At Ak Lu'um Waldorf School, we have committed ourselves to this, and we believe that it is fundamental to consider two aspects in order to achieve this understanding: the study of anthroposophical principles and also knowledge of what stands behind the native "cosmovisions" and cosmogonies that we seek to understand in the light of spiritual science.

For this reason, and considering that not all members of a Waldorf school have the same interests, time, and facility to study anthroposophy, we have focused on a topic that is both an everyday part of school life and also a subject that is constantly studied and relatively easy to digest, namely the cycle of the year and its festivals.

We are also fortunate to work with members of our community interested in the native cultures of Mexico, our region, and specialists who have been studying these cultures for years.

Through combining these two realities, we have managed over the years to impregnate our celebrations of the cycle of the year with the native culture, and particularly to celebrate a whole festival with the archetypal impulse of the Mesoamerican peoples: The Autumn Equinox Festival.

The Cycle of the Year and Waldorf Schools

In Waldorf education, school life, from early childhood through high school, is framed by the cycles of nature, the cosmic forces that envelop the earth and, from the Mystery of Golgotha, by the spiritual impulses that flow from these forces.

This is clearly seen in the daily rhythm of the classrooms or homes, which are transformed, season after season, not only in their colors and textures, as seen on a seasonal table or blackboard drawings, but also in the songs, verses, and rounds that we hear inside them.

But it is the celebrations and festivals that most strongly indicate the time of the year we are living in; they not only serve as a guide for children to understand that we live within an annual rhythm—that after Advent, Christmas will arrive, and so on—but it refers us directly to the animistic interiority of the human being and to the processes that live in our development as individuals and as humanity.

To explain this more easily, let's draw and study the following scheme.

In Figure 1, we can clearly see that there is a relationship between the daily cycle of nature, the earth's yearly cycle, and what the human being experiences in the course of life. As mentioned above, reference could also be made to the Christ impulses that permeate humanity, but they divide the year into three parts (a trinity) rather than four (paralleling the traditional four seasons) , and will not be discussed here.

Within the annual cycle there are multiple divisions, markers, and celebrations that are associated with specific aspects of life, such as agriculture, religion, and even

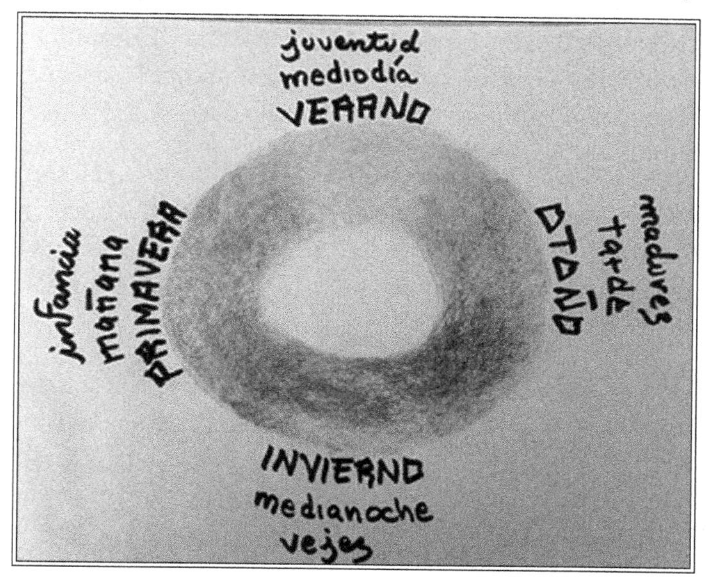

Figure 1. English Translation: The green (left) section of the color wheel represents infancy, morning, and springtime; the yellow (top), youth, noontime, and summer; the red (right), maturity, afternoon, and autumn; and the blue (bottom), winter, midnight, and old age.

initiatory systems. In this article, however, we will focus on the so-called equinoxes because they mediate all the rest.

Already the word *equinox* gives us a clue to its meaning. It comes from the Latin word *aequinoctium*: from *aequus*, equal, and *nox*, night. So, the word refers to something that is or lasts the same length as the night; we know that this is the day, since that is the time during which most of the beings of the earth live their lives. We have two moments every year, the autumn and spring equinoxes, where the duration of day and night are the same. These differ from the solstices. *Solstice* comes from the Latin word *soltitium* (*sol sistere*: still sun), which marks the moments where the sun is at the most extreme points of its movement, the "longest day of the year" in the summer, and the "shortest day" in the winter.

These moments are very obvious to us and, in modern times, are something to which we do not give much importance. However, for the human being of antiquity, these were not only relevant moments that marked seasons of hunting, gathering, and later planting and harvesting, but they came out of a long process of observation and recording through which we became aware of them. Awareness of these times of the year came out of the human nature to ask inherent questions about their origins, the functioning of nature, and humanity's place in the world. As human beings improved their ability to observe and record, they developed an understanding of the cycle of the year.

It was the observation of the movement of the sun across the celestial vault and its constant appearance and disappearance over the horizon that gave rise to the most profound and complex answers about the origin and functioning of nature, as well as the place of the human being and the earth within it.

The light and heat produced by the sun was always considered the foundation of life and the manager of the natural rhythms on the planet. This was true to such an extent that in the past, the human being only reproduced in one season like the rest of nature (fertilization in summer and births in the spring).

The knowledge about the movement of the sun with respect to the earth is so old and complete that the first post-Atlantean civilizations already knew about the so-called precession of the equinoxes, which produces changes, barely perceptible by human beings, in the moments that the sun rises and sets.

This apparent movement of the sun over the surface of the planet is the result of the slow and gradual change in the orientation of the earth's axis, which has a cycle of 25,776 years. The length of this cycle shows not only the importance of and interest in understanding the movements of the sun, but also the value of constant transmission, generation after generation, of the recording and understanding of this phenomenon.

Having established the importance of the equinoxes for human civilization and the cycle of the year, let us return to what spiritual science tells us about how to understand these moments of the year.

Rudolf Steiner ([1909] 1972) reminds us that the human being lives between the polarities of all the colors and that it is the work of the human soul on earth to achieve a balance within these colors. This work of the human soul contributes to the continuous development of the whole cosmos.

In this way, and returning to our previous scheme, we can locate the "poles" which govern the annual cycle—the solstices, either the extreme of the longest day, with the hottest season on one side, or the other extreme, the shortest day or longest night, with the coldest season on the other. We know from the descriptions in *Occult Science* (Steiner [1909] 1972) how, like breathing, in winter the earth inhales and in summer, it exhales.

However, when it comes to describing the midpoints, the explanation becomes more complex, and refers not to a maximum point, but to the long processes of the loss and gain of light and heat.

Here is a question that will illuminate our way: If on the dates of both equinoxes, the length of the day is the same as the night, what is then the difference between these two equinoxes in the qualities of light and heat, the quantity being the same?

The answer is simple, but it becomes profound when Steiner reminds us that in order to understand one polarity, we must always consider the other and always consider that one goes to and comes from the other and vice versa.

Our artwork will show us how at the two midpoints (equinoxes), between the extreme poles (solstices), light and heat become different in their quality, because one comes from light and goes towards darkness (autumn equinox) and the other comes from darkness and goes towards light (spring equinox).

Artistic Work

On a sheet of paper in landscape orientation, draw a yellow stripe on the top and a dark blue stripe on the bottom, with each stripe occupying a third of the sheet and leaving a white third between them. On the right side of the paper, between the two stripes, use red to represent the midpoint between yellow and blue; let the red disappear into the darkness of the blue. On the left side, use green as the midpoint between yellow and blue, and let the darkness of the green become lost in the brightness of the yellow. It is important that you leave a white circle in the center of the sheet.

How is the light different at each equinox (where red and green fade into blue and yellow)?

How do you feel the gain and loss of heat?

What does it mean to go into the darkness from the light?

What does it mean to go into the light from the darkness?

What is in balance, if each side of the scale is different in quality, but not in quantity?

With this exercise we reflect that although in both equinoxes the amount of "sun" is the same, its light and heat have important differences that

affect our understanding of the cycle of the year and even more for understanding the animistic work of the human being to balance his life between polarities.

Mesoamerican Myths and Anthroposophy

For this section of our study, I must remind you that it is not the objective of this workshop to learn about iconography or pre-Hispanic American philosophy, since these are specialties that require a vast amount of recording and analysis.

The author has been working on understanding the cosmovision and cosmogonies of Mesoamerican peoples for more than twenty years and has been involved in anthroposophy for more than ten years. This article the fruit of that work, which will in the future become his master's thesis in art history at the Universidad Antonoma de Yucatan, but does not explain the full process by which he reached his conclusions. He is happy to share further information, and invites all interested to contact him personally through WECAN.

Nor will we deal here with Rudolf Steiner's thoughts about America, its spiritual impulses, and its place in the development of mankind, because it would divert us from our goal.

The purpose of this article is to share the Mesoamerican archaeological symbolism about the cycle of the year, particularly the autumnal equinox, in order to give a real example of how native culture can be integrated into the annual festivities. And here we come to the heart of this discussion.

Just twenty years ago, within the academic circles that study ancient American cultures, there was a debate about whether the "myths" can be valid sources of knowledge for the understanding of these cultures, or whether they are only whims and literary figures that have come down to our days.

Today, except for a few archaeologists who disagree, anthroposophists and others agree that the myths and narratives that were transmitted orally for centuries and then written down are an indispensable source for understanding these peoples, mainly because of the almost total destruction of their culture and original texts.

Likewise, and as a result of the exhaustive and methodical work of anthropologists and historians, a "hard core" of archetypes has been recognized and shared by all American peoples, from Alaska to Patagonia.

This hard core has shown that in all native narratives, iconography, and astronomical interpretations, there is a symbolic constant that allows us to recognize a unique archetypal origin that only varies in terms of geography and its social and ecosystem specifications; we can, therefore, use the mythical images of one group to understand and expand the vision of another and vice versa.

For this reason we can take as a basis a narrative of Wixarikas (self-named; the culture is more widely known as Huichole) origin. This group still exists in the Mexican Republic. The Wixarikas story can help with the study and analysis of other myths of more ancient origin—Otomi, Quiche, Aztec, Zapotec, Itza and Totonaca, for example—to complete a picture and even form a real basis for understanding archetypes.

Thus the story of the Blue Deer, which is still told by the old shamans in Western Mexico and is the basis for an annual pilgrimage of hundreds of miles across the desert, is brought to life and nurtured by these diverse cultural traditions. It is born anew in the light of Spiritual Science, as it is tied, through the archetypal images, to the concepts of the universe, the earth, and the human being that Rudolf Steiner offers us.

First, we start with the origin of the human being and his home, the earth. We can consider the evolution of the earth as part of the cosmos, which as anthroposophy explains, developed together through several epochs. This development can be seen in multiple myths throughout America, but we can summarize it in the following table:

Period	Main Light/ Celestial Being	Type of Material/ Terrestrial Being	Gestated Kingdom/ Body
First Sun	Cloud	Clay	Mineral/physical cycle
Second Sun	Aurora/Dawn	*Teocintle* (first corn)	Vegetable/etheric cycle
Third Sun	Morning star/ Venus	Deer	Animal/astral cycle
Fourth Sun	Sun	Human	Human being/"I"

Figure 2. The earth's evolutionary periods and their representation

Prior to the appearance of what is explained in Figure 2, the American people recognized that "All was in darkness and emptiness" until two forces united to gestate, to create or develop, all that exists. Drawing on images in nature, they could symbolize the creation of the earth with the images in Figure 3.

The sphere of water and air represents earth/feminine/matter/mother, and the meteorite of earth and fire approaching earth symbolizes

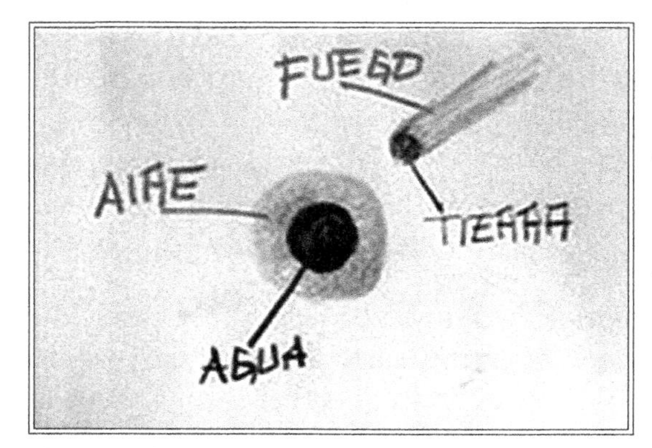

Figure 3. English translation: agua, water; aire, air; fuego, fire; tierra, earth

heaven/male/spirit/father/serpent. These two creative forces, dualities of the same origin, unite as do ovum and sperm to create everything.

However, as explained above, earth's creation has been the result of several periods in which it evolves and is constantly transformed by heaven. We have this image not only in America, but also in the Asia, where these forces appear as the tiger and the dragon, and in ancient Egypt with the lion and the cobra.

But let us return to Figure 2 to understand the story of the Blue Deer, remembering that objects of observable nature are being used to symbolize archetypal moments.

The first section of the table indicates evolutionary periods. We translate it as sun, but the words cycle, day, or time could be used as well. In Spiritual Science there are four cycles until the appearance of the human being.

The second section indicates how the being gestated by these two forces is seen in the celestial vault. It is a light that, as it becomes more consistent and palpable, can be observed by the beings on earth. The faintest light was the *via lacteal* (the Milky Way), which they called the cloud serpent. Then came the light of dawn or the *alba*, to give way to the morning star, and finally to the *sol* (sun).

Since the third epoch, this observation directed the gaze of terrestrial beings towards the east.

The third section tells us what material was created during that period, or who was the main being gestated by these two forces on earth—for example, first sun and cloud begat clay; third sun and the morning star begat the deer. It takes us back to the ancestral myths of human creation throughout America, where the first human was created from mud. This first human could not even stand upright and looked more like an air bubble on the earth's surface, so it was decided to destroy it and create the second human. This being was still made of mud, but with an internal structure of *teocintle* reeds (wild corn). But although these humans could stand up, they were not sentient and kept colliding with each other, so it was decided to destroy them and create the third human. This human was given the consciousness of the stars and became wise, although capricious and vain like the deer (our older brother). The third humans did not understand by whom they had been created and fell into sin, so it was decided to destroy them and create the fourth humans, who had bodies of clay, the inner strength of *teocintle*, stellar passion, and for the first time, an individual conscience that gave them the potential to not only transform themselves and their environment, but to recognize the forces that had created them and to try to be worthy of them.

The fourth section simply points out what I have already explained in the third section and demonstrates the equivalence with spiritual science.

So now, let's go back to the Blue Deer and to the key moment of our story: "The sun had hidden for the first time." We can understand this by referring to Figure 3 and recognizing that in the fourth cycle, both the sun and the human being appeared for the first time. That first morning in the story, where the sun rose over the horizon in the east, symbolized the childhood of the present humanity, and the spring for the earth, as we saw in Figure 1.

When midday came, the human being reached full creative power, youth, and the earth experienced summer, but after the sun reached its zenith, it began to descend towards the west and its light and heat lessened.

When the human being entered the period of maturity, the earth entered its autumn. Finally, the sun touched the horizon again, but this time on the opposite side from where it had risen before; the light and heat of the sun disappeared almost completely.

The food that had been plentiful during the spring and summer became scarce, and the humans feared that darkness would reign over them, as they knew that was the original state of the earth.

The most experienced female human being, *la abuela* (grandmother; in Mayan the word *ix*, means woman, shaman, and jaguar), sent for the "younger adult" beings, to entrust them with the search for food.

They came down from their "central" mountain, or earthly navel, and headed towards the place where they had seen the sun rise, the east.

They were faint with hunger and had not yet found any food when the Blue Deer, their older brother, appeared to them from the ashes (*ocaso*). (According to Spiritual Science, humanity perceived the things that produced pleasant emotions and images in blue tones in the third period.) The Blue Deer guided them through the flat desert to the entrance of a cave in the far east of the earth.

There the deer disappeared and the four humans, who already showed signs of full maturity and weariness, decided to follow him to the darkness of the cave. Inside, they were surprised to find a warm chamber (*utero*; uterus) that was as luminous as the sun (*sol*), where the Blue Deer waited to give them four ears of a new food. (The corn consumed today was the fruit of four different processes of human selection and hybridization since the *teocintle*, or first corn, and that gave rise to the agricultural, sedentary lifestyle in America.)

The four human beings, already showing the first signs of aging, returned by the same path to their original mountain as the last glow of the sunset still faintly illuminated the earth, and they were able to give their community a food that the grandmother knew how to transform and prepare.

This food possessed the two original creative forces that would nurture and gestate a new beginning for human beings. It possessed the solar forces of the father and the earth forces of the mother.

The only condition for the use of this food, which the Blue Deer transmitted to the "young ones" at the moment of granting them the precious gift, was that they should take care of it and preserve it generation after generation; and that they should never forget its origin. Otherwise, the darkness of winter and old age would take them to an eternal, cosmic night in which there would be no possibility of being reborn.

For this reason and after centuries of doing so, the Wixarikas continue to tell the "younger ones" this story, so that they do not forget that after the darkness the light will come again, as long as we remember our celestial origin and take care of the terrestrial food that sustains us.

This is the reason why in Ak Lu'um we want to keep this promise to our big brother: the Blue Deer.

References

Steiner, Rudolf. (1909) 1972. *An Outline of Occult Science*. Great Barrington, MA: SteinerBooks.

The Blue Deer

A traditional legend of the Wixarikas (Huichol) people of Mexico

This legend talks about the moment of the first "autumn" on earth. In the beginning of times there was a long moment of darkness before the Sun appeared in the sky for the first time. For that reason, when the first afternoon happened, people were worried because they didn't know if the sun would come out again. They were scared to be in the dark again and without any food.

The Deer promises that the corn will take care of them during the time of darkness if, during the time of light, people take care of the corn by planting, harvesting, preparing, and cooking it. The grandmother is

able to teach this process, as the Deer was in fact her first grandchild, a half "big brother" to the human being. For this reason, the Wixarikas people used to call the Deer Big Brother.

A long time ago, when the sun hid beneath the horizon for the first time, the people were scared and suffered from terrible diseases, droughts, and hunger that struck the earth.

That's when the venerable grandmother decided to send four young men to hunt; their task was to find and bring food to share with the community. The young men represented the four elements: earth, air, water and fire.

The young men left wearing bows and arrows. The days went by and the young men couldn't find food anywhere, until one night, when they were lighting a fire to go to sleep, a robust and beautiful deer jumped through the flames.

In that moment, the young men were already tired, but the love for their community made them strong enough to go hunting, so they followed the beautiful beast.

After a long time of chasing it, the deer felt mercy for the young men and allowed them to rest. On the next day, the deer showed up again in front of the young men and they started to chase after it once again.

The deer was leading the young men to the House of the Sun, from where the sun came out the first time.

When the young men and the deer met on top of a cliff, the deer jumped through a cave, to the place where the Spirit of the Earth lived. The young men ran to the place, but they couldn't find the deer again.

Soon after that, one of the young men shot an arrow at what he thought was his prey, the deer, but when they went closer to see what he'd shot, they only found a crack in a rock. They decided to go through it.

The young men were genuinely surprised when they found themselves in a big and bright place that seemed to shine as bright as the sun. In the middle of this big place were four ears of corn: one red, one white, one yellow, and one blue. The young men knew that the corn was meant to be for them, a gift from the deer to help them save their town.

The young men went back and offered the new food to the grandmother. The grandmother prepared it and presented it to the community in the shape of a golden sun, warm and nutritious, our tortilla that helps people to survive through the cold and difficult season, while we wait for the sun to appear above us once more.

Adaptation for the Early Childhood Home or Classroom

Mariana Espinosa

A long time ago in a faraway town, when the sun set for the first time, the people were very worried because all of the food ran out.

Then a wise grandmother decided to send four young men to search for food to share among the community.

The young men were very brave. They walked for days and nights, looking for something to eat. Time passed by and they couldn't find

anything—until one night, when they were lighting up a fire to go to sleep, a robust and beautiful deer jumped through the flames. The young men starting chasing after it, but the deer was too fast, and they couldn't reach it.

After a long chase, the deer stopped and allowed the young men to catch up to it. On the next day, the deer showed up again and the young men starting chasing after it once more. When the young men and the deer reached a cliff, the deer went in a cave and the young men went after it but couldn't find it. One of them shot an arrow and made a hole in one of the stones. When they looked into the hole they found in the center four ears of corn: a red one, a white one, a yellow one, and a blue one.

The young men took the corn back to their town and the wise grandmother prepared it and presented it to the community in the shape of a golden sun, warm and nutritious, that will help the people to eat while they wait for the sun to shine above them once more.

Working with Stories

Reimagining the World of Story

Stephen Spitalny

I want to take a moment to recognize that the land on which I am living is the unceded territory of the Awaswas-speaking Uypi Tribe. The Amah Mutsun Tribal Band, composed of the descendants of Indigenous people taken to missions during Spanish colonization of the Central Coast, is today working to restore traditional stewardship practices on these lands and heal from historical trauma.

My wish is to get you all to think and decide for yourselves what it is you want to do. My impatience and enthusiasm sometimes make it seem like I know the one and only way. I apologize in advance for that. My hope is that you end up with more questions than answers that you can wrestle with long into the future. I am passionate about Waldorf education and have high hopes for its potential to change the world.

This article is about reawakening the world of story. We all need stories. We rely on stories. We tell stories about ourselves. Sometimes stories get stuck and prevent change. One part, the first part of our work as teachers, is to discover ourselves. Who am I? What are my own stories? What stories do I tell others? What stories do I tell myself? And this work includes revealing our biases to ourselves. We can't change unless we own that we have work to do on ourselves.

To quote the late Margret Meyerkort: "What right do I have to stand before the children if I do not develop myself?"

So, inner work is our primary task—developing ourselves, the tool with which we stand before the children. *Mindful of Race* by Ruth King (2018) is a powerful study guide for examining important aspects of bias and perspective. Don't just read it, do the work, do the exercises for your own sake, and for the children.

Then there are other kinds of stories, stories of imagination. Of course, the storytellers and story creators are also revealed in those. We all need a chance to imagine a reality different from our own, and in so doing possibly learn something.

Our children need to dream, to visualize, to create inner pictures so they can find their destiny and prepare for the contributions they will one day make to our world. To focus, to concentrate, to pay attention, and to think "outside the box" are capacities that need to be protected and nurtured in children, especially now when children's minds and senses are being overstimulated by the external world's ever-present electronic images.

What stories support the children in coming into the world as it is changing and evolving and becoming, and what stories support the children's becoming? How can we use story intentionally as a healing element? We can heal the world one heart at a time. What images do we want to offer to the children? Storytelling is an intimate opportunity, a direct link, into the developing will, psyche, and neurology of the children in our care.

A foundational thought of Waldorf education is that we support the children toward revealing their gifts for the world, even though we have no idea who they are or who they will become. Therefore we must support the children in developing their own sense of identity without the obstacles of our biases so they become secure in their own sense of self. It is from this sense of self that all exploration of the world begins. The children interact with the world and eventually offer their gifts to the world.

The biases of teachers and parents get in the way of the children embracing and expressing their own uniqueness. Our goal is to support each child's developing sense of wholeness, which entails an integration of the multiple parts of their identity.

When we tell stories to young children, one consequence is that the children's inner landscape becomes populated with archetypes and images that will accompany them throughout their lives and help them form their own identities. That presents us with a big responsibility.

Stories speak on various levels at the same time: at the symbolic or esoteric level; through archetypes; and through images of the physical world.

It is time for a serious look at the stories we tell young children and a sharpening of the focus of our lens for detecting embedded messages and images that don't meet our values.

In this day and age, it is especially important to consider how cultural dominance and racist stereotypes, as well as shaming, blaming, and punishment, have crept into stories. These messages do not resonate with our intentions of creating a future world of compassion, love, and harmony.

I want to focus on one particular type of story—the so-called fairy tale. Fairy tales ask, Who am I? And what can I expect on my path of incarnation?

A fairy tale is a true story told in imaginative pictures that tells of each individual's soul/spirit development. It is a symbolic representation of the struggle to become whole and free. Fairy tales are spirit-truth in image form, they are true, imaginative pictures of the soul's and spirit's reality and transformation. And they are a most important nourishment for the soul.

In many fairy tales, you can still sense the ancient origin. And in the distant past, these stories were part of an oral tradition from a time when humanity was more closely connected to spirit and nature.

Stories, especially fairy tales, are received by the soul, by the heart—not by intellect. The nourishment of fairy tales is a seed of moral strength. We receive pictures of strength and determination to carry through, to overcome evil, to see that it is not always the more clever and older ones who are best suited to the tasks, and so on.

Interpretation of these stories is an intellectual activity. We must use our heart to see if our intellect is telling the truth. The story speaks for itself; interpreting stories with the children deprives them of the richness of the images.

Once upon a time, when I first traveled the road toward becoming a Waldorf kindergarten teacher, it was commonly advised not to mess with fairy tales, not to change them because they are ancient wisdom encapsulated in story form. I accepted that and later even sometimes admonished students in courses I taught not to change those fairy tale gems from the past.

The archetypes we find in fairy tales are universal. However, these archetypes manifest in, or through, different cultures and, therefore, have different "flavors."

Fairy tales are, in fact, are symbolic representations of received spiritual wisdom which, when originally created, perhaps only an initiate had the credentials to modify. That wisdom had been received by various shamans, initiates, and the like, from the imaginal sheath that surrounds the earth. These wisdom stories were received by wise and spiritually opened people all over the world, and through them, the spiritual archetypes incarnated into the flavors and tastes of the culture of which the initiate was a member. What the stories share is the truth of the striving to become a whole human being of body, soul, and spirit. The stories are rich in symbology and can be decoded by recognizing the archetypes and extrapolating to the various aspects of the developing human being.

In the long-ago times, these stories were told around the fire, at the hearth. They were told to adults to give them tools for their own future development. First told by wandering bards, minstrels, shamans, and so on, the general public received these stories and began to pass them on, as well as to embellish and enhance the stories. Each story evolved based on the regions it traveled through and on the style and culture of the tellers. The stories offered seeds for enlightenment and possibilities for gathering strength and moral fiber to face the challenges of their own lives.

These wisdom stories are populated by ordinary-seeming people who prevail against obstacles in their path, usually placed there by those with more power than they have. There are usually elements of cleverness, compassion, or courage that are required for the resolving of the obstacles. In the plot and characters of the story, one can discover many aspects of the human being. I think of each character and situation within a story as aspects and experiences of an individual human being. All the characters are inside all of us. These stories do not depict outer physical reality, rather they give pictures of inner development, images of the path of becoming truly human and uniting the various aspects of ourselves, and pictures of the functioning of the human body.

At the dawn of the age of materialism, at the beginning of the era of the printing press, the ancient wisdom tales began to be collected and entombed in the printed word. What had been living, evolving story-beings, now became codified. They became lifeless corpses of their former selves. Before being printed, these "fairy stories" were a "rolling literature" (Warner 2016), and they could and would be infinitely adapted and modified. The age of materialism could not accept these wisdom tales as having value, and in industrialized societies, the term "fairy" stories arose to belittle these powerful tales and to announce that they were at best fit for children.

I have a great passion and a deep personal connection to so-called fairy tales from many countries all around the world. I collect collections of stories and hungrily peruse the contents searching for ones that I connect with and that bring forth the images I want to offer the children.

I think it is essential that a teacher offer stories in which the physical images meet the diversity of the world around us. People from everywhere are everywhere. And, if one thinks that reincarnation is a possibility, or a reality, people from everywhere have been "otherwhere" before.

There are five continents, innumerable islands, approximately two hundred countries, and uncountable, unique cultures. To help make this world a better place, let's all learn some stories outside of our familiar story comfort zone!

Often, we can discover a connection to stories of our own family ancestors. What about stories that arose on the local land on which we stand?

While fairy tales do not depict physical reality, the images they contain can perpetuate stereotypes of disempowerment and can create and perpetuate implicit biases. Many, but not all, of the traditional European fairy tales have young, male heroes. What if we made sure to create a balance between male and female heroes, between young and old characters who become the one that succeeds? Does the wicked person always have to be an old woman or a stepparent? We need to explore the old stories and be sure for ourselves that the images do not perpetuate unhealthy stereotypes, while at the same time making sure the stories message the values for which we stand.

To do this, we have to do our own personal open-minded exploring, and we have to be open to listening to the thoughts and experiences of others who may have different perspectives, including parents and colleagues. For help, we can refer to the fifth of Steiner's "Six Basic Exercises" (Steiner [1910] 1997).

Consider some common descriptions of people in published fairy tales: beautiful princess; handsome, golden haired; the marriage between male and female characters, and so on. These descriptions are worthy of deep consideration and possible revision. It is up to each one of us to wake up to hidden messages within these stories and choose accordingly. What about our own gender biases? How does that manifest in our choices of stories?

What about our puppets? What skin colors should we use? I don't have to decide about skin color, because for many years I have chosen to represent the characters in colors that relate to how I think about the human's bodies. Perhaps the youngest daughter, the one who will succeed, who for me represents the will, is clothed in red and has a red face (not pink). Or the elder, who is a healer in the story, is clad in green with a green face. Or the character symbolizing the consciousness soul is golden skinned with golden yellow clothes. You get the idea.

I have often heard a complaint from parents and adult students that the endings of the stories are too harsh, the retribution excessive. And I have explained those complaints away, first, by mentioning that the story is a depiction of a spiritual reality and is not meant to be thought of as a physical reality. Second, I have often quoted British essayist and mystery writer G. K. Chesterton, who wrote in 1922 about the magnitude and violence of these retributions, "children are innocent and love justice; while most of us [adults] are wicked and naturally prefer mercy."

And still I have wondered. We are teaching the children *on many levels* when we tell a story. I have come to a place where I think it is important that we offer examples of compassion and nonviolent resolution. If we continually offer violent retribution as the resolution or redemption in stories, then where goes hope for compassion and peace in the world? I think it is high time to find and tell stories that offer compassion without violence and punishment, stories that picture kindness and justice.

Somewhere along the way, perhaps one or two hundred years ago, the "rolling literature" of stories came upon an obstacle which hindered its growth, development, and enhancement. It is time to get the ball rolling again. I think stories are longing for their infinite updates. It is time to rewrite fairy tales, or better, to allow them to live again.

In our time, it seems more important than ever that we teach compassion and hope, offer stories where love triumphs over evil without violent punishment for misdeeds. It is time to hear stories of different family constellations that reflect the reality of children with two moms or two dads. There are evils of our time, and perhaps they differ from those of the past. There is an unhealthy focus in today's culture on physical form and beauty and an idealized version of perfection. Can we help to counter that with images of inner strength and wisdom and integrity, and leave off descriptions of outer physical form? Can we bring stories to encourage love and protection and creative solutions for our planet and the life on it which faces rising challenges and risks of extinction? Embedded in many stories are images of power structures and racial bias that we need to become aware of and, through our retelling, undo their inherent racism! To do this, we can:

- Penetrate through the imaginal language of the story to the underlying archetype and truths.
- Identify the elements of the story that do not serve your values.
- Make changes to serve your values while staying true to the spiritual messages conveyed by the story.

I am not suggesting we go over each of the polished gems and old standbys and rework them for political correctness. I am not suggesting a free-for-all of redoing the classics to make them more palatable. The various media have done that, and I think it didn't go very well and is generally not very satisfying. What I am suggesting is to consider if changing certain aspects could in fact enhance a story while keeping true to its underlying spiritual messages.

One classic story I edited is the story of "Jorinda and Joringel" from the Grimms' collection (Grimm 1983, tale 69). It is a story that has always been both an attraction and a mystery for me. I changed it so the girl rescues the boy. Nancy Mellon spurred me on. She suggested that the wicked old woman could be a wicked old man. And she too appreciates that in this story about disenchantment, the blood red flower simply makes it impossible for the wicked man to do magic anymore, without further punishment.

It is so important to offer images to everyone about the possibilities inherent in their humanness. Flexibility in relation to the old stories is particularly important in our current stage of human cultural development. In my adaptation, the boy and girl have been renamed, the girl must free the boy from his enchantment, and the wicked old woman has become a man. The story follows this article.

In the closing lecture of the foundational course for the first Waldorf teachers in 1919, Rudolf Steiner pointed to the importance of filling ourselves with the power of imagination (Steiner [1919] 1995). Steiner said that it is equally important that the imaginations are true. If the imaginations the teachers are teaching from are true, then the teacher must have the courage to rely on those imaginations, the courage to be free and independent in thinking and still unite themselves with true imaginations instead of false. The teacher must, therefore, have courage for the truth. And this courage for the truth which the teacher develops must go hand in hand with a feeling of responsibility towards checking the truth of imaginations.

It is time to write new stories. And it is time to set the old stories free.

References

Chesterton, G. K. 1922. "Of Household Gods and Goblins." http://www.gkc.org.uk/gkc/books/goblins.html. Accessed September 7, 2022.

Grimm, Jacob and Wilhelm. 1983. *Grimms' Tales for Young and Old: The Complete Stories.* Translated by Ralph Mannheim. New York: Anchor Books.

King, Ruth. 2018. *Mindful of Race: Transforming Racism from the Inside Out.* Louisville, CO: Sounds True.

Steiner, Rudolf. (1910) 1997. *An Outline of Esoteric Science.* Hudson, NY: Anthropsophic Press.

———. (1919) 1995. *Study of Man.* Forest Row, UK: Rudolf Steiner Press.

Warner, Marina. 2016. *The Short History of the Fairy Tale.* Oxford, UK: Oxford University Press.

Yasmeen and Yousef
A retelling of "Jorinda and Joringel" by the Brothers Grimm

Adapted by Stephen Spitalny

There was once an old castle in a great, dense forest. A wicked old man lived there by himself. In the daytime, he turned himself into a cat or a night owl, and at night he resumed his human form.

He had a way of luring birds and animals, and when he had killed them, he would boil or roast them. If anyone came within a hundred steps of the castle, they froze in their tracks and couldn't stir from the spot until he said certain words that broke the spell. If a young boy went inside the circle, the man turned him into a bird and shut him up in a wicker cage that he carried to one of the rooms in his castle. He had about seven thousand of these rare birds, all in wicker cages.

Now once there was a girl named Yasmeen, who was as clever and curious as any in all the world. Her dearest companion was a kind boy named Yousef. Their greatest joy was in being together. One afternoon they went walking into the forest. "Take care," said Yousef, "don't go too near the castle." It was a lovely evening, the sun shone between the tree trunks and lit up the green darkness of the forest, and the turtledoves sang mournfully in the old beech trees.

Now and then Yasmeen wept. She sat down in the sun and sighed, and Yousef sighed too. They were as sad as if death were near. They looked around in bewilderment, for they no longer knew the way home. The sun was still half above the hill and half below it. Yasmeen looked through the bushes and saw the old castle wall only a few steps away. She was overcome with dread. Yousef sang:

My little bird with the wing so red sings sorrow, sorrow, sorrow.

He sings that the turtledove is dead, sing sorrow, sor . . . jug, jug, jug.

Yasmeen looked at Yousef. He had been turned into a nightingale and was singing, "jug, jug, jug." A night owl with fiery eyes flew out of the forest and around Yasmeen, and screeched three times: "To whoo, to whoo, to whoo." Yasmeen couldn't move; she stood still as stone, unable to speak or move hand or foot. The sun had gone down; the owl flew into a bush. A moment or two later, a gnarled old man, stooped and scrawny, came out of the bush. He had big red eyes and a crooked nose which almost touched his chin. Muttering to himself, he caught the nightingale in his hands and carried it away. Yasmeen couldn't say a word or stir from the spot and the nightingale was gone. At last, the man came back and muttered: "Greetings, Zachiel. When the moon shines on her, let her go." And Yasmeen was free. She fell to her knees and begged the old man to release Yousef, but the man said Yasmeen would never see him again and left her.

She cried out, she wept, she moaned, but all in vain. "Oh, what is to become of Yousef?" Yasmeen went away and came at last to a strange village. There she stayed a long time, guarding the sheep. She often walked around the castle, but not too close. Then one night she dreamed she had found a blood-red flower with a fine, large pearl in it. She plucked the flower and went to the castle with it. Everything she touched with the flower was freed from the spell. She also dreamed that the flower helped her to free Yousef.

When she awoke the next morning, she began to search hill and dale for the flower. Eight days she searched, and early on the morning of the ninth, she found the blood-red flower. In the middle there was a big dewdrop, as big as the finest pearl. Holding the flower, she journeyed day and night until she reached the castle. When she came to within a hundred steps of the castle, she was not held fast and continued on to the gate. Her heart leaped. She touched the gate with the flower and it sprang open. She went in, passed through the courtyard, and listened for the sound of the birds. At length she heard them. On and on she went till she found the room, and there was the wicked man feeding the birds in the seven thousand cages. When he saw Yasmeen, he was angry, very angry. He scolded, he spat poison and gall at her, but he couldn't get near her, not within two paces. Paying no attention to him, Yasmeen went up and down the rooms looking at the birds in the cages. There were hundreds of nightingales. How would she ever find Yousef?

Suddenly, while she was searching among the birds, she saw the old man, on the sly, taking down one cage and heading for the door with it. In a flash, Yasmeen jumped and touched the cage with the flower. She also touched the old man, who then lost his power to do magic. And there stood Yousef next to Yasmeen, as human as ever. After she freed all the others from the spell, Yasmeen and Yousef went home, and they lived happily for many, many years.

Inclusive Storytelling in the Waldorf Early Childhood Classroom

Chris Shaw

My journey as a Waldorf teacher began twenty-six years ago when I brought my children to the Waldorf kindergarten. The Waldorf school inspired our home life and my parenting, and eventually led me to pursue a career in Waldorf early childhood education.

What I did not consider at that time, nor for many years, was that my experience of the Waldorf school was not a universal experience. It was a largely white, Eurocentric, heteronormative experience. In fact, many of the ways Waldorf education spoke to me actually excluded, offended, and even traumatized Black and Native children and families and children and families of the global majority.

I can recall a Black mother who enrolled her child in one of my children's kindergarten classes. I remember thinking she was loud, but I cannot remember what she said, because I didn't actually listen to her. I remember thinking she was angry, although I know I never spoke with her. When that Black mother withdrew her Black child, I did not ask why. I thought I knew why. I thought they left because she was angry and that her child did not behave. I never thought about why she might be angry or if she even actually was angry. What did she feel and experience? I have no idea because I ignored her and judged her child's behavior according to my own skewed understanding of what I found "appropriate." My judgment of this family was based solely upon my own bias and lack of understanding. For years, I never once considered the deep loss our community suffered each and every time a family of color made the difficult decision to pull their child from our school.

For years I have failed, as a Waldorf parent and teacher, to look at myself and ask why Native and Black American families don't find community in our school. I and others have said things like, "We don't have Black students because there are no Black people around here," and made harmful assertions that link race, class, and socioeconomic status. I have heard the assumption voiced that a Black person who comes to our school will be commuting from one of the more densely populated, lower income, urban centers, even though we are all very aware that there are more than five different colleges and universities with many Black teachers, staff, and students all within a twenty-minute bus. As a school, we have failed to ask what it is about us that makes this place inaccessible.

As a movement, we have a lot of work to do, and we have been fortunate for the benevolence the spiritual world provides. After all, the angels brought us Keelah Helwig. Last night, Keelah made herself vulnerable and encouraged all of us to be vulnerable. But getting vulnerable is not easy. When I consider my personal behavior and biases, I feel ashamed and embarrassed, and I don't like to look at the harm I have caused. However, as a white educator working to welcome Black children into my predominantly white classroom, I must do all I can to unlearn my bias and racist ideas. The ability to be vulnerable is essential. If Keelah can do it, we can do it; if Keelah encourages us to be vulnerable, then we must.

In my first year teaching, I was given a class of fourteen beautiful children. One of the children, Gabriel, had dark brown skin, black hair, and beautiful, deep-brown, sparkling eyes, just like his mama. His papa was white. Mama was the head heart surgeon at a large local hospital. In my class, Gabriel was surrounded by all of the stories and images Keelah spoke of; peach-skinned, golden-haired children doing all of the most wonderful things. Gabriel had to tolerate choosing from dolls and toys that looked like his playmates and teachers, and not like himself, his beloved older sister, his mama, nor any of his close-knit, loving, beautiful extended family.

Gabriel loved the colors and textures in our classroom. He was gentle, kind, and sensitive. His playmates loved him and the peace he generated in play. When Gabriel's family chose public school for him and I knew it wasn't a financial choice, I made the deeply erroneous assumption that this powerful, well-educated, progressive, wealthy family was choosing public school for the academics and in order to assimilate. I was sad that they did not know better and that Gabriel would miss out on a wonderful education that would nourish him—and our school grew whiter.

A couple of years after Gabriel left my class, I was at an all-school open house when a beautiful Black Mother and her two Black sons appeared in my classroom. I say they appeared because I did not notice them entering. The boys went right to work, playing together in the kitchen area. They were busy, absorbed, and creative. While they were there, I was engaged in conversation with a handful of white parents who had much to say and many questions to ask, while my assistant tended to their children and tried to keep our classroom in relative order.

At the end of the event, our enrollment director came in to usher everyone out of my classroom and on to the next thing, and everybody filed out. That was when I took notice of that beautiful mama sitting there on the rug, holding the space for her children to play but now quietly directing them to tidy their playthings. I saw her and asked, "Do you have any questions?" She smiled kindly, looked me in the eye, and slowly shook her head. "No," she said. "Okay," I replied and went back to tidying all of the toys the white parents had apparently forgotten to ask their white children to tidy away. When the Black family started to leave, I said, "Goodbye, thank you for coming," and again that loving and attentive mother looked right at me, smiled, and said, "Thank you for having us," and they left.

As they left, I thought, "I wonder why she didn't have any questions? Why would she bother to come here and not say anything or ask any questions?" I looked around at the now empty classroom and saw the hand-felted wall hangings depicting those same peach and gold children Keelah told us about. Every doll and toy, every book, every image, aside from one token dark-skinned baby doll, represented a little white child. Finally, I asked myself, why would she have any questions? What would she ask?

Why are you choosing to beautify this room only with pictures of white children?

Why didn't you greet me when I came in?

Why didn't you introduce yourself to us as you did with the white families?

Why didn't you show any interest in my beautiful children?

Are you racist?

And each would be a totally valid question.

I had to ask myself, why? And I found the answer right there inside of me, right there where it had been all along. Right there alongside all of the other stereotypes and assumptions, in a great big pit dug into the very center of my being. The answer was that I felt uncomfortable. That I had not had an opportunity to love Black people, and I was protecting myself from saying or doing something wrong. I had lived on this earth for fifty years and had not cultivated one authentic relationship with a Black person. That was why.

I would like to say that this was a turning point, but it was not. It would still take another entire school year and a direct and brave conversation with two white parents from my class for me to make some real changes. Those white parents came to me and told me very clearly that I needed to change and the school needed to change if they were going to send their white child into the grade school. They told me I needed to do anti-racism training and that their white child needed to be in a school where all children are seen and loved and valued, where their child would have the opportunity to have friends who are Black, teachers who are Black, to be in community with people who are Black, and to love Black people. And finally, thankfully, I heard them.

Changing the dolls and images is easy, and it must be done. Add some books by Clifton Taulbert to your book basket and take down your Sistine Madonna. Put up some of the pictures currently available from WECAN and check out the Montessori supplies site for others. Make Black puppets. Dark Black, not tan, with big curly afros. Nova sells a nice dark brown skin fabric that I love. Look inward and do the work you have to do to see your own bias. If you are white and don't see any bias, keep looking. You are sure to find it in there somewhere. Undoing bias and choosing an anti-racist path takes effort, but there are some wonderful people and organizations like Alma Partners, the People's Institute for Survival, and beyond, as well as many local organizations that can help.

Once we begin to undo our internalized racism and create an authentic space for Black families, families of color will come to our schools, and when they come, we must be prepared. We cannot wait to do this work. This movement can no longer afford to contribute to the pain and trauma felt by Black people when they meet Waldorf education, and we teachers must take responsibility for that. We must educate ourselves and work to change ourselves from the inside out in order to meet these children and families and practice the radical empathy bell hooks often spoke about—the same radical empathy Keelah, Meggan, and Joaquin demonstrated for us just last night.

Where to begin? The following list of resources might be a good place to start.

Recommended Resources

Alma Partners. https://www.almapartners.net/.

Hamad, Ruby. *White Tears/Brown Scars: How White Feminism Betrays Women of Color.* New York: Catapult Publishing, 2020.

Love, Bettina. *We Want to Do More Than Survive.* Boston: Beacon Press, 2019.

The People's Institute for Survival. https://pisab.org/.

Smith, Clint. *How the Word is Passed.* New York: Little, Brown and Company, 2023.

Exploring Picture Books
as a Tool for Building Spaces Where All Children Are Celebrated

Rie Seo

We started our workshop by exploring our reactions and responses to the phrase, "books in Waldorf early childhood classrooms." We wanted to explore any successes or challenges together. What stirs up inside us when we think of bringing picture books into our classrooms? Resistance? Confusion? Excitement? I was pleasantly surprised to hear lots of excitement! There was also a great sense of relief in the group for openly talking about books with our Waldorf colleagues. Many of us felt that it had been taboo to bring books to Waldorf EC classrooms—or even to talk about them. But we are doing it now!

My Journey

It was at a WECAN conference in 2021 when I heard that colleagues in other Waldorf schools had been using books in their classrooms. To be honest, I was confused. I couldn't imagine how they used the books with the children or what kind of books were okay. I didn't even know where to start. I also felt deep resistance inwardly. Though in the past, we had made recommendations for parents to read certain "Waldorf classics" at home, and we had used them sporadically in the extended care program at our school, we were taught to believe that books were not our teaching tools in Waldorf EC classrooms. Why haven't we used them in the classroom before, and why is it okay now?

Then some of my EC colleagues at our school started to use books in the classroom—I was surprised a bit, but also saw that it could be done beautifully, and the children were okay and even seemed to enjoy it.

My teaching partner, Maria Kata, and I thought, "Should we use books? Could we?" But we didn't know where to begin! Then around Diwali this past school year, our colleague Lisa Miccio showed us a small book with beautiful pictures and said she had read it with her children. So we decided to give it a try. We wanted to honor the Diwali tradition and felt like the book was the right way to do it. At story time, Maria lit a candle, held up the book with great care, read some parts as she showed the pictures, and also added her own words. The mood created was as sacred as our usual story time, and the children seemed to take in the words and images deeply.

While we remain cautious not to abuse books or heavily rely on them, we have gradually become more open to exploring their possibilities. Although we still do mostly spoken stories and puppet plays for our story time, we also have our "book look" time and bring in carefully selected books for special occasions. We have also used books such as *Pink Is for Boys* (Pearlman 2018) to bring different perspectives from those that had been strongly living in our class community. We also shared our book journey with our parents, which led to a series of meaningful conversations. We experienced many ways that books could help cultivate what had been missing in our classrooms.

We began to search for more books we could potentially bring to our classroom. When I looked at the fairy tale book section of our local library, a little store at our school, and our postcard collection in the classroom, I was very disappointed. There was very little diversity in the images they presented. It hit me that this was how it had always been in the Waldorf world, and that we need to be more proactive about bringing different images to young children. We need to actively create and plant seeds so that more diverse imaginations can bloom. How and what can we change?

Why Do We Need Diverse Books and Images?

Why can't we stick to those traditional, beautiful books we had been using? As Meggan Gill beautifully shared with us in her keynote, there is a danger in a single story. A single story does not offer the truth.

Citing a TED Talk by author Chimamanda Ngozi Adichie, the Mackin Community explores the problem of the single story. "[Adichie] explains, 'The single story creates stereotypes, and the problem with stereotypes is not that they are untrue, but that they are incomplete. They make one story become the only story.' Adichie points out that we must seek diverse perspectives and, in turn, writers must tell their own stories. 'Telling the stories that only we can tell, about our experiences, hopes, and fears, helps break down the power of cliches and stereotypes'" (Tessman 2018).

Statistics

Images courtesy David Huyck, Sarah Park Dahlen, and Molly Beth Griffin. Used under Creative Commons License 4.0. These images can be viewed in greater detail online by doing a search for their titles.

This is what has been available in the world of children's books over the past several years. There is an improvement in seeing more children of color represented, but we need to see more.

Mirrors, Windows, and Sliding Glass Doors

Dr. Rudine Sims Bishop beautifully describes why we need more diverse representation (Reading Rockets n.d.). She speaks beautifully about the concept of mirrors, windows, and sliding doors. Here is an excerpt from Dr. Bishop's interview:

We need diverse books because we need books in which children can find themselves, see reflections of themselves. I wrote a piece, maybe 1990 it was published, which I called "Mirrors, Windows, and Sliding Glass Doors" [see a link to this article in the resource list]. And I think that's really why we—children need to see themselves reflected.

But books can also be windows. And so you can look through and see other worlds and see how they match up or don't match up to your own. But the sliding glass door allows you to enter that world as well. And so that's the reason that the diversity needs to go both ways. I mean it's not just children who have been underrepresented and marginalized who need these books.

It's also the children who always find their mirrors in the books and, therefore, get an exaggerated sense of their own self-worth and a false sense of what the world is like because it's becoming more and more colorful and diverse as time goes on.

> **Mirrors** *are visual representations that reflect different aspects of children's identities, including family, gender, race, ethnicity, culture (such as special traditions, celebrations, songs, nursery rhymes, and games), language and how language is used, religion, socio-economic status, immigration experience/status, and other aspects of identity and lived experiences.*
>
> **Windows** *are the visual representations where children see aspects of a world different from their own. Window books offer a glimpse into other people's lives and introduce readers to new worlds, perspectives, and experiences; allow readers to develop new interests; and remind readers that their view is not the only view.*

> **Sliding glass doors** *are the visual representations that invite us to walk into a story and become part of the world created by the author. Readers become fully immersed in another experience and become engaged with important topics and social issues; the author invites the reader to move beyond looking in a mirror or window; and the books invite readers to enter into and have an inner view of a different world. The messages conveyed are often more explicit.*

These concepts have helped me immensely in how I imagine my classroom, not only with regard to books but to any other visual elements children see. The idea of sliding glass doors especially offered me a new and strong perspective. I had struggled to bring books that highlighted differences even to my own children at home for fear of damaging their view that the world is good. But as I began to see some books as sliding glass doors, they became important and powerful. I now see them as a tool that provides views into a world different from mine. Sliding glass doors invite us to feel and think. They go beyond just looking in a mirror or window. They encourage us to enter into and engage with a diverse world.

Practical Examples

We have three kindergartens, and each room has a collection of books. It started organically, and my classroom was the last to join. We have a basket of books and also display a particular book or two depending on the season or theme on the table. How do we use them?

Book Look. This is the time when children choose books to look through on their own without us reading to them. In our classroom, it happens organically without an assigned date or time. In winter, we came indoors more often due to cold weather, and we used those little pockets of time when we had to be inside to have a "book look" time. Some children look at the pictures intently, and some children talk to their friends and share what they see. Some children make up their own stories based on the images and tell them to themselves and friends. Overall, I sense that there is something special and joyful in looking through books together as a group.

Story time. As I shared earlier, we used a book about Diwali to introduce the festival to the children. For Thanksgiving, our intention was to bring a more diverse, true perspective of the occasion and pay our deep respect to the native people who have been taking care of our land for a long, long time. I took inspiration from a book called "The autumn equinox, celebrating the harvest" and turned it into a *kamishibai* style of storytelling. *Kamishibai*, literally "paper theater" in Japanese, is a form of storytelling that combines a set of standard-size illustrated paper cards paired with a scripted performance by a narrator. (Please see the list of resources for more on kamishibai.) That was accompanied by our Thanksgiving story, circle, and performance of African dance by our high school seniors, which is our school's tradition. For Martin Luther King Jr. Day, to honor who he was and what he achieved for us, we came up with a story inspired by a book called *Happy Birthday, Martin Luther King Jr.* by Jean Marzollo, illustrated by Brian Pinkney (1993). At the end of the story, we showed the book's cover. Various books about him and his achievements were displayed on our book table as well.

At our parent meeting. We brought the topic of DEIJ (diversity, equity, inclusion, and justice) work in general to our class meeting and discussed examples of how we were creating a more diverse environment for children through many aspects of our work, including books. The parents looked through the books from our classroom, which led to a meaningful discussion. We were grateful that our parents were open and eager to carry the same approach both at home and at school. We are in the process of building a better classroom library with the class fund that our parents have donated.

How Do We Select Books?

I found it is easier to choose if I think in terms of a few categories and will share them as a starting point. The first two questions we ask ourselves in choosing books are:

- Are they beautiful, imaginative, and authentic?
- Do all the children and families in our class find themselves and their friends reflected?

We might also ask:

- Are the books for classrooms?
- For lending library and home recommendation?

Books for the Classroom

I try to find books that are mirrors and windows; celebrations of daily life featuring children of the global majority; about the seasons, our work and chores, exploration and play; about festivals; less focused on particular differences or challenges that children of color experience.

How do the children read the books?

Books for children to look through on their own. Are the pictures beautiful, imaginative, and authentic? What mirrors and windows does the book offer? Are the pictures safe to look at without being accompanied by an adult's words/context?

Books to read together with adults—as a group or individually. Are the pictures and the story beautiful, imaginative, and authentic? What mirrors and windows does the book offer?

Books for lending library and home recommendation. Do they offer diverse perspectives? Do they address what's living in the class community? Are they beautiful, imaginative, and authentic? What mirrors, windows, and sliding glass doors do the books offer?

For lending library and home book recommendations, I try to find the books that are sliding glass doors—books that more explicitly offer opportunities to experience inside perspectives of people who are different from people who the children are familiar with. (these books may need more time and space for children to ask questions); books that actively replace stereotypical images in fairy tales; and folktales from diverse cultures.

I hope that what I have shared here offers a good starting point to begin exploring your journey with books and images. How can we bring more diverse images—through books or any other way? How can we actively create mirrors, windows, and sliding doors for those you serve? What do you see yourself changing in your practice?

> *Remember that consciousness is power. Consciousness is education and knowledge. Consciousness is becoming aware. It is the perfect vehicle for students. Consciousness-raising is pertinent for power, and be sure that power will not be abusively used, but used for building trust and goodwill domestically and internationally. Tomorrow's world is yours to build.*
>
> —*Yuri Kochiyama (Tajiri and Saunders 1993)*

References

Marzollo, Jean. 1993. *Happy Birthday, Martin Luther King Jr.* Illustrated by Brian Pinkney. New York: Scholastic Press

Reading Rockets. N.d. "A Video Interview with Rudine Sims Bishop, PhD." https://www.readingrockets.org/teaching/experts/rudine-sims-bishop. Accessed August 24, 2022.

Tajiri, Rea and Pat Saunders (dirs.). 1993. *Yuri Kochiyama: Passion for Justice.* Documentary film.

Tessman, Katy. Nov. 14, 2018. "Building a Diverse Book Collection: Providing Windows, Mirrors, Sliding Glass Doors, and Beyond." Mackin Community. https://www.mackincommunity.com/2018/11/14/building-a-diverse-book-collection-providing-windows-mirrors-sliding-glass-doors-and-beyond/.

Additional Resources

Adichie, Chimamanda Ngozi. "The Danger of a Single Story." TED video. TED Global, 2009. https://www.ted.com/talks/chimamanda_ngozi_adichie_the_danger_of_a_single_story.

Bishop, Rudine Sims. "Mirrors, Windows, and Sliding Glass Doors." Reading Is Fundamental, (1990) 2015. https://scenicregional.org/wp-content/uploads/2017/08/Mirrors-Windows-and-Sliding-Glass-Doors.pdf.

———. Interview. Reading Rockets. YouTube video playlist, 2015. https://youtube.com/playlist?list=PLLxDwKxHx1yLH9i0wFT21xxYSSMjS4KGi.

Chenoweth, Robin. "Rudine Sims Bishop: 'Mother' of Multicultural Children's Literature." Ohio State University College of Education and Human Ecology, September 5, 2019. https://ehe.osu.edu/news/listing/rudine-sims-bishop-diverse-childrens-books.

Flores, Tracy, Sandra Osorio, and Colorín Colorado. "Why Diverse Books Matter: Mirrors and Windows." ¡Colorín colorado!, 2021. https://www.colorincolorado.org/article/why-diverse-books-matter-mirrors-and-windows.

———. "How to Find Diverse Books." ¡Colorín colorado! https://www.colorincolorado.org/article/how-find-diverse-books. Accessed August 23, 2022.

Kamishibai. http://www.kamishibai.com. Accessed August 23, 2022.

Myers, Walter Dean. "Where Are the People of Color in Children's Books?" *New York Times*, March 15, 2014. https://www.nytimes.com/2014/03/16/opinion/sunday/where-are-the-people-of-color-in-childrens-books.html.

Reading Rockets. Transcript from an Interview with Rudine Sims Bishop. https://www.readingrockets.org/books/interviews/bishop/transcript#mirrors. Accessed August 24, 2022.

Booklists from the EC Classrooms of the Waldorf School of Garden City

The following are links to Goodreads lists created for early childhood teachers and families. All were most recently accessed on August 24, 2022.

Celebration of Life. https://www.goodreads.com/review/list/93549898-rie?ref=nav_mybooks&shelf=wsgc-celebration-of-life.

Around the Festivals. https://www.goodreads.com/review/list/93549898-rie?ref=nav_mybooks&shelf=wsgc-festival.

Sliding Glass Doors. https://www.goodreads.com/review/list/93549898-rie?ref=nav_mybooks&shelf=wsgc-sliding-glass-doors.

Fairy Tales/Folk Tales. https://www.goodreads.com/review/list/93549898-rie?ref=nav_mybooks&shelf=wsgc-fairy-tale.

More Books!

The following links are to Goodreads lists created for WECAN teachers and families. All were most recently accessed on August 24, 2022.

Celebration of Life. https://www.goodreads.com/review/list/93549898-rie?ref=nav_mybooks&shelf=wecan-celebration-of-life.

Around the Festivals. https://www.goodreads.com/review/list/93549898-rie?ref=nav_mybooks&shelf=wecan-festival.

Fairy Tales/Folk Tales. https://www.goodreads.com/review/list/93549898-rie?ref=nav_mybooks&shelf=wacan-fairy-tale.

Sliding Glass Doors. https://www.goodreads.com/review/list/93549898-rie?ref=nav_mybooks&shelf=wecan-sliding-glass-doors.

Additional Resources

Alma Partners (https://www.almapartners.net/)

The following resources provide introductions and supplements to topics covered in this book: antibias education, storytelling "windows and mirrors" for considering representation in early childhood curricula, racial identity development, cultural appropriation and appreciation, and a glossary of terms. All of these resources should support teachers and parents in conversing with each other and the children in their care about race and racism in and out of the classroom. Alma Partners compiled this list and glossary in 2021.

Anti Racist Post. "If you don't understand cultural appropriation, imagine working on a project and getting an F and then somebody copies you and gets an A and credit for your work." Instagram post. January 8, 2021. https://www.instagram.com/p/CJyx2Dhg4Op/.

Avins, Jenni, and Quartz. "The Dos and Don'ts of Cultural Appropriation." *The Atlantic*. October 20, 2015. https://www.theatlantic.com/entertainment/archive/2015/10/the-dos-and-donts-of-cultural-appropriation/411292/.

Derman-Sparks, Louise, and Julie Olsen Edwards. "Conversations that Matter: Talking with Children About Big World Issues." National Association for the Education of Young Children (NAEYC), May 21, 2020. https://www.naeyc.org/resources/blog/conversations-that-matter.

———. "Understanding Anti-Bias Education: Bringing the Four Core Goals to Every Facet of Your Curriculum." NAEYC. Originally published in *Young Children* 74, no. 5 (Nov. 2019). https://www.naeyc.org/resources/pubs/yc/nov2019/understanding-anti-bias.

Helms, Janet E. *Black and White Racial Identity: Theory, Research, and Practice.* Westport, CT: Greenwood Press, 1990.

PBS Learning Media. "Culture, What You See and What You Don't." Lesson plan for grades 6–8. https://ny.pbslearningmedia.org/resource/e0dddf26-fc83-4178-9db3-5f3a3eeee2f5/culture-what-you-see-and-what-you-dont/#.WbmOeMiGMuU. Accessed September 14, 2022.

PBS Teachers' Lounge. "The Importance of Windows and Mirrors in Storytelling." November 5, 2020. https://www.pbs.org/education/blog/the-importance-of-windows-and-mirrors-in-stories.

Poston, W. S. Carlos. "The Biracial Identity Development Model: A Needed Addition." *Journal of Counseling & Development* 69, no. 2 (1990), 152-155. https://doi.org/10.1002/j.1556-6676.1990.tb01477.x.

Shabazz, Barbara. "Culture isn't something that people do or have to be cute, fun, or interesting." Instagram post with slideshow. May 8, 2021. https://www.instagram.com/p/COnUnLvjZCW/.

Tatum, Beverly Daniel. "Talking about Race, Learning about Racism: The Application of Racial Identity Development Theory in the Classroom." *Harvard Educational Review* 62, no. 1 (Spring 1992). https://equity.ucla.edu/wp-content/uploads/2017/01/Tatum-Talking-About-Race.pdf.

———. *Why Are All the Black Kids Sitting Together in the Cafeteria?* New York: Basic Books, 2017.

Racial Identity Development: Five Stages of Development for BIPOC and People of the Global Majority (Tatum, "Talking about Race")

Pre-encounter: The individual seeks to assimilate and be accepted by whites, and actively or passively distances themself from other persons of their own race. This de-emphasis on one's racial/group membership may allow the individual to think that race has not been or will not be a relevant factor in one's own achievement.

Encounter: Movement into this phase is typically precipitated by an event or series of events that force the individual to acknowledge the impact of racism in one's life. Faced with the reality that they cannot truly be white, the individual is forced to focus on their identity as a member of a group targeted by racism.

Immersion/Emersion: This stage is characterized by the simultaneous desire to surround oneself with visible symbols of one's racial identity and an active avoidance of symbols of whiteness. Individuals in this stage actively seek out opportunities to explore aspects of their own history and culture with the support of peers from their own racial background.

Internalization: In this stage, secure in one's own sense of racial identity, there is less need to assert the "Blacker than thou" or similar attitudes often characteristic of the immersion/emersion. One's attitudes favoring one's racial identity become more expansive, open, and less defensive. The internalized individual is willing to establish meaningful relationships with whites who acknowledge and are respectful of their self-definition. The individual is also ready to build coalitions with members of other oppressed groups

Internalization/Commitment: Those in this last stage have found ways to translate their personal sense of race into a plan of action or general sense of commitment to the concerns of their own race as a group. This is sustained over time. Race becomes the point of departure for discovering the universe of ideas, cultures, and experiences beyond one's own race, in place of mistaking one's race as the universe itself.

Biracial Identity Development (Poston)

Personal Identity: The biracial individual experiences a sense of self unrelated to ethnic grouping; this occurs during childhood.

Choice of Group: As a result of multiple factors, individuals feel pressured to choose one racial or ethnic group identity over another. Society requires individuals to say, "I am" in a way that fails to recognize biracial identity.

Categorization: The individual's choices are influenced by status of the groups with which they identify, by parental influence, cultural knowledge, and appearance.

Enmeshment/Denial: The biracial individual experiences guilt and confusion about choosing an identity that isn't fully expressive of all their cultural influences; denial of differences between the racial groupings; possible exploration of the identities that were not chosen in the choice of group and categorization stages.

Appreciation: The biracial individual comes to appreciate the possibility of multiple identities.

Integration: The individual experiences a sense of wholeness, integrating multiple identities.

Six Stages of White Racial Identity Development (Helms)

Contact: The white individual experiences A lack of awareness of cultural and institutional racism, and of one's own white privilege. This stage often includes naive curiosity about or fear of people of color, based on stereotypes learned from friends, family, or the media. Those whose lives are structured so as to limit their interaction with people of color, as well as their awareness of racial issues, may remain at this stage indefinitely.

Disintegration: Increased interaction with people of color or new information about racism may lead to a new understanding, which marks the beginning of this stage. In this stage, the bliss of ignorance or lack of awareness is replaced by the discomfort of guilt, shame, sometimes anger at the recognition of one's own advantage in being white, and the acknowledgement of the role of whites in maintaining a racist system. Attempts to reduce discomfort may include denial or attempts to change significant others' attitudes toward people of color. Societal pressure to accept the status quo may lead the individual from the disintegration to the reintegration stage.

Reintegration: At this point, the desire to be accepted by one's own racial group, in which the overt or covert belief in white superiority is so prevalent, may lead to a reshaping of the person's belief system to be more congruent with an acceptance of racism. The guilt and anxiety may be redirected in the form of fear and anger toward people of color who are now blamed as the source of discomfort. It is easy for whites to become stuck at this stage of development, particularly if avoidance of people of color is possible.

Pseudo-Independent: Information seeking about people of color often marks the onset of this stage. The individual is abandoning beliefs in white superiority, but may still behave in ways that unintentionally perpetuate the system. Looking to those targeted by racism to help them understand, the white person often tries to disavow their own whiteness through active affiliation with persons of color. The individual experiences a sense of alienation from other whites who have not yet begun to examine their own racism, yet may also experience rejection from persons of color who are suspicious of his or her motives. Persons of color moving from the encounter to immersion phase of their own racial identity development may be particularly unreceptive to a white person's attempts to connect with them.

Immersion/Emersion: Uncomfortable with their own whiteness, yet unable to be truly anything else, the individual may begin searching for a new, more comfortable way to be white in this stage. Learning about whites who have been antiracist allies to people of color is an important part of this process. Whites find it helpful to know that others have experienced similar feelings and have found ways to resist the racism in their environments, and they are provided with important models for change.

Autonomy: The internalization of a newly defined sense of self as white is the primary task of this stage. The positive feelings associated with this redefinition energize the person's efforts to confront racism and oppression in daily life. Alliances with people of color can be more easily forged in this stage because the person's antiracist behaviors and attitudes will be more consistently expressed.

The Culture Iceberg

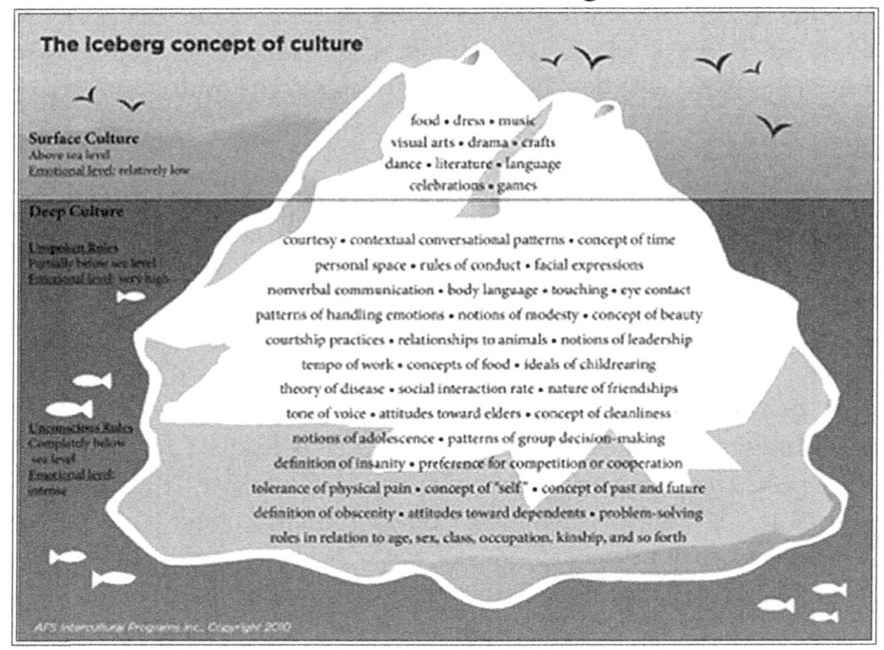

Glossary of Terms

Sources for these definitions include the National Association of Independent Schools, the Kirwan Institute for the Study of Race and Ethnicity at The Ohio State University, Lakeside School, and Dr. Beverly Daniel Tatum's *Why Are All the Black Kids Sitting Together in the Cafeteria?*

Anti-racism: "Anti-racism is the active process of identifying and eliminating racism by changing systems, organizational structures, policies and practices, and attitudes, so that power is redistributed and shared equitably" (NAC International Perspectives: Women and Global Solidarity).

Cultural appropriation: Theft of cultural elements for one's own use, commodification, or profit—including symbols, art, language, customs, and so

PBS Learning Media, https://ny.pbslearningmedia.org/resource/a353a4ba-cd56-4999-97dd-0e40e11a7211/iceberg-concept-of-culture-images-and-pdfs/#.Wa7Yech94uU on—often without understanding, acknowledgement, or respect for its value in the original culture. Results from the assumption of a dominant culture's right to take other cultural elements.

Cultural responsiveness: The application of a defined set of values, principles, skills, attitudes, policies, and behaviors that enable individuals and groups to work effectively across cultures. Cultural responsiveness is a developmental process (and continuum) that evolves over time for both individuals and organizations. It is defined as having the capacity to: (1) value diversity; (2) conduct assessment of self; (3) manage the dynamics of difference; (4) acquire and apply cultural knowledge; and (5) adapt to diversity and the cultural contexts of the communities in which one lives and works.

Diversity: The presence, acceptance, and appreciation of varied cultures. The concept of diversity embraces the wide range of human characteristics used to mark or identify individual and group identities. These characteristics include, but are not limited to, ethnicity, race, national origin, age, personality, sexual orientation, gender, class, religion, ability, and linguistic preferences. Diversity is a term used as shorthand for visible and quantifiable statuses, but diversity of thought and ways of knowing, being, and doing are also understood as natural, valued, and desired states, the presence of which benefit organizations, workplaces, and society.

Equity: A condition that balances two dimensions—fairness and inclusion. As a function of fairness, equity implies ensuring that people have what they need to participate in school life and reach their full potential. Equitable treatment involves eliminating barriers that prevent the full participation of all individuals. As a function of inclusion, equity ensures that essential educational programs, services, activities, and technologies are accessible to all. Equity is not equality; it is the expression of justice, ethics, multi-partiality, and the absence of discrimination.

Ethnicity: A social construct that divides people into groups based on characteristics such as shared sense of group identity, values, culture, language, history, ancestry, and geography.

Gender: Socially constructed categories of masculinity and manhood, femininity and womanhood that go beyond one's reproductive functions. Gender is distinct from one's sexual orientation.

Gender expression: This is the way we show our gender to the world around us through such manifestations as clothing, hairstyles, and mannerisms, to name a few.

Gender identity: A person's internal sense of themselves as a specific gender. A cisgender person has a gender identity consistent with the sex they were assigned at birth. A transgender person has a gender identity that does not match the sex they were assigned at birth. Gender, however, is a spectrum and is not limited to just two possibilities. A person may have a nonbinary gender identity, meaning they do not identify strictly as either a boy or a girl.

Implicit bias: The attitudes or stereotypes that affect our understanding, actions, and decisions in an unconscious manner. These biases, which encompass both favorable and unfavorable assessments, are activated involuntarily and without an individual's awareness or intentional control. Everyone is susceptible to implicit biases.

Inclusion: Encompassing all; taking every individual's experience and identity into account and creating conditions where all feel accepted, safe, empowered, supported, and affirmed. An inclusive school or organization expands its sense of community to include all, cultivating belonging and giving all an equal voice. Inclusivity also promotes and enacts the sharing of power and recognition of interdependence, where authorizing individuals and community members share responsibility for expressing core values and maintaining respect for differences in the spirit of care and cooperation.

Microaggressions: Microaggressions are subtle words, cues, behaviors, or any combination of these that insult, invalidate, or exclude traditionally marginalized group members. The long-term effect of microaggressions can be a significant negative effect on one's health.

Multiculturalism: The presence of many distinctive cultures and the manifestation of cultural components and derivatives (e.g., language, values, religion, race, communication styles, and so on) in a given setting. Multiculturalism promotes the understanding of and respect for cultural differences, and celebrates them as a source of community strength. Multiculturalism is also defined as a set of programs, policies, and practices that enable and maximize the benefits of diversity in a school community or organization.

Privilege: Systemic favoring, enriching, valuing, validating, and including of certain social identities over others. Individuals cannot "opt out" of systems of privilege; rather these systems are inherent to the society in which we live.

Race: A social construct that divides people into groups based on factors such as physical appearance, ancestry, culture, history, and so on; a social, historical, and political classification system.

Racism: A system of advantage based on race. This advantage occurs at the individual, cultural, and institutional levels. Racism can also be defined as prejudice plus power.

Sexual orientation: A concept referring to a person's sexual desire in relation to the sex/gender to which they are attracted; the fact of being heterosexual, homosexual, bisexual, asexual, or pansexual.

Social class (as in upper class, middle class, working class): Refers to people's socioeconomic status, based on factors such as wealth, occupation, education, income, and so on.

Restorative justice: A theory of justice that emphasizes repairing the harm caused by criminal behavior. It is best accomplished through cooperative processes that allow all willing stakeholders to meet, although other approaches are available when that is impossible. This can lead to transformation of people, relationships, and communities.